Health Care Administration

A Quantitative Research Study on Afghan American Nurses, Leadership, and Acculturation Factors

BELAL A. KAIFI, Ph.D., Ed.D., M.P.A., M.B.A.

Breezeway Books

ISBN: 978-1-62550-6139

Printed in the United States of America

Dedication

I dedicate this research study to my four boys. As a first-generation Afghan American,

your father is doing his best to provide better opportunities for all of you.

Acknowledgements

This research project would not have been possible without the guidance, patience, and feedback from my esteemed colleagues (Dr. Carlos Cardillo, Dr. Sharon Nazarchuk, and Dr. Patricia Rhynders). Furthermore, I would like to thank some of my mentors over the years: Dr. Farid Younos, Dr. Bahaudin Mujtaba, and Dr. Marina Aminy. I owe all of you a great debt of gratitude for inspiring me to strive for excellence. Finally, I would like to thank my wife, children, and family for all of their love and support over the years.

Torn Between Cultures: An Afghan American Woman Speaks Out
(2003)

By: Dr. Maryam Qudrat Aseel, Ph.D.

- *"Afghans who were fortunate enough to escape Afghanistan with their lives had to overcome tremendous social, economic, and spiritual struggles. Their perfectly good lives were entirely disrupted. They abandoned their homes and all their possessions, enduring being thrust into the socialization process in foreign lands, and had to raise children who were less connected to or interested in their beliefs"* (p. 45).

- *"Traditionally, men were the breadwinners and women were the caretakers"* (p. 4).

- *"American and Afghan cultures are so disparate that there seemed to be no hope for marrying the two. This left only one choice, to shift completely toward one value system or the other"* (p. 68).

- *"I have lived an Afghan-American life, a hyphenated life that does not fit fully into any social category; deeply embedded in me lie two value systems that have grown to signify polar extremes, those of the East and West"* (xiii).

Abstract

Background: The impact of acculturation on leadership style is an important topic for the global community. Acculturation is one of the frequently used variables in career development research because of its significance to many aspects of career development for immigrants. As of 2019, no research on Afghan American registered nurses (RNs) working in the US healthcare system existed in the literature.

Objective: The goal of this investigation was to learn about the perceived leadership style of Afghan American registered nurses who work in the US healthcare system based upon a number of acculturation factors. The variables of interest in this study were *sex*, *generation*, *work experience*, and *acculturation levels* to see their influence on perceived leadership style.

Design: A quantitative, non-experimental, descriptive-correlational design using primary retrospective data (the actual data needs to be here) was employed in this study.

Results: The results showed that task-oriented leadership correlated significantly with American acculturation, years of nursing experience, and participant sex. Task-oriented leadership was most strongly associated with the male sex, followed by years of nursing experience, generation, and Afghan acculturation. Relationship-oriented leadership correlated significantly with all five predictor variables (American acculturation, Afghan acculturation, generation, nursing experience, and participant sex), whereas relationship-oriented leadership was predicted by acculturation and sex.

Conclusion: Implications, limitations, and directions for future research were discussed. Due to the constantly changing nursing field and high demand for healthcare administrators, nursing curriculum should emphasize the importance of leadership skills. Hospitals should consider implementing more training courses and opportunities for nurses to develop their leadership skills. Future researchers should consider comparing American nurses with Afghan American nurses among similar nursing settings and with similar job titles.

Keywords: Afghan American, registered nurse, acculturation, leadership, culture.

Table of Contents

List of Tables

List of Figures

"If we knew what it was we were doing, it would not be called research, would it?"

~ Albert Einstein

"We cannot always build the future for our youth, but we can build our youth for the future."

~ Franklin Delano Roosevelt (FDR)

"Career advancement was a distant goal [for Afghan refugees], and became something that parents eventually wished for their children rather than for themselves."

~ Maryam Qudrat Aseel

"A nation's culture resides in the hearts and in the soul of its people."

~ Mahatma Gandhi

Chapter I: Introduction

The United States is known as a melting pot or as the land of opportunity. As a result of immigration, individuals from all over the world have settled in the United States. According to the most current data available, it is estimated that nearly 44 million immigrants from Europe and the Oceanic countries live in the United States (Zong, Batalova, & Hallock, 2018). When entering the US, each individual brings unique traditions, cultures, and customs to this land of opportunity. Non-native health field workers are making the workforces more culturally diverse, although in the United States, about 60 percent of new entrances into the job market are expected to be from the dominant culture: white, native born Americans (Tjosvold & Leung, 2016). The focus of this study was Afghan American nurses practicing in the US health system.

Acculturation is one of the frequently used variables in career development research because of its significance to many aspects of career development for immigrants. According to Miller and Kerlow-Myers (2009), acculturation has been linked to a number of important career outcomes such as job choice and satisfaction, performance reviews, career decision self-efficacy, and occupational stress. Tang (2019) explains that low acculturated individuals might experience more struggles in career development because they try to fulfill their roles in a society with different values and expectations than their traditions. In addition, Tang (2019) further states that acculturation is an important factor for the career development of immigrants and minority members and needs to be considered for its impact on one's career. Miller and Kerlow-Myers (2009) encourage researchers to use bilinear multidimensional measures (e.g., ARSMA-II) or assessment protocols when interested in assessing acculturation.

The purpose of this descriptive correlational quantitative study was to explore the predictors of leadership style of Afghan American nurses based on a number of variables such as *sex*, *generational identity*, *acculturation*, and *nursing experience* by evaluating the differences in scores on the Leadership Style Questionnaire and the Acculturation Rating Scale (Cuéllar et al., 1995; Northouse, 2004).

Background

The issue addressed in this study was focused on the dilemma facing immigrants and refugees settling in the United States, which is how much of their culture should they or can they maintain and still be able to function in their professional fields among the dominant culture. Historically immigrants will settle in communities where others from the same country reside (Hirschman, 2013). In this way, they have support from one another and are also able to maintain their culture and their value systems. Issues of acculturation and career development are particularly prevalent among those who choose to work in service type systems such as schools and medical facilities where they are engaged with people from many cultures but the majority of people served remain part of the dominant culture (Aseel, 2003; Emerson, 2007; Lu et al., 2016). For example, length of residence and mainstream language usage in the host country contribute to the development of different acculturation strategies (Lu et al., 2016). In particular, the population of immigrants in this study are from Afghanistan who provide direct patient care as registered nurses in the US healthcare system.

Researchers have attempted to examine the dominant leadership orientation of individuals from different contexts because of the implications for cross-cultural management, individuals who are expatriates, the repatriation process, and to help provide awareness and understanding of different cultural norms among individuals living and working in a global community (Mujtaba & Balboa, 2010; Mujtaba, 2010; Nguyen et al.,

2

2014; Tajaddini & Mujtaba, 2011). One half of the PhDs working in the US are foreign-born, as are 45 percent of the physicists, computer scientists, and mathematicians (Fisher, 2005; Wright, 2013). At the same time, more and more American employees are working as expatriates who staff offices in foreign countries.

Despite the plethora of information on leadership, researchers have pointed out that there is much that we do not know (Judge et al., 2004; Mujtaba, 2009; Nguyen et al., 2014; Northouse, 2004). There are myriads of potential variables and mediators that could be investigated in regard to leadership because organizations depend upon leaders to influence followers to achieve a common goal. The variables of interest to this study included *sex*, *generation*, *work experience*, and *acculturation level*.

Contemporary researchers have recommended comparing years of experience to see if this is a variable influence on the task and relationship scores of respondents (Mujtaba & Balboa, 2009). Mutaba (2010) explains that the research can be broadened to include part-time and full-time employees to see if task and relationship scores differ. Nguyen et al. (2011) discusses the importance of future researchers examining task and relationship orientations across cultures to see if there is a similarity or difference among cultures. Mujtaba et al. (2013) highlights the need for future researchers to analyze leadership style based upon different training backgrounds, age, and level of education to see if these variables influence task and relationship orientations.

Chen and Van Velsor (1996) pointed out that there is only a limited knowledge base in regard to leadership behaviors pertaining to nontraditional and non-western leaders. Years later, as research on culture and leadership developed, Snaebjornsson et al. (2015) noted that all cultures have different expectations of leaders of the two sexes that potentially influence their actions and behaviors. Sociological research generally agrees that men and women do have some biologically determined differences, but sexes are socially constructed and

3

culturally embedded, or perceived differently in different cultures (Collard & Reynolds, 2005; Fletcher, 2004; Rudman & Glick, 2010; Schmitt et al., 2017). Snaebjornsson et al. (2015) point out the dire need for additional research on cross-national studies in which researchers concentrate on sex and leadership.

Problem Statement

The general problem is non-native healthcare workers are often caught between two worlds: deciding to assimilate into the dominant culture of the United States or to maintain their culture, which often results in personal familial and workplace struggles (Aseel, 2003; George, 1993; Ludwick & Silva, 2000). Furthermore, there is an increased demand for healthcare administrators because of the aging US population and as a result, there will be 72,100 additional jobs for healthcare administrators by 2026 (Bureau of Labor Statistics, 2018). The population under study is first-generation Afghan American nurses practicing in the US health system. The specific problem addressed in this study was identifying the acculturation variables that influence relationship and task-oriented leadership styles. The information can potentially help prevent obstacles and barriers for Afghan American nurses seeking promotions, administrative positions, and career advancement working in the US healthcare system (Aseel, 2003; Heggertveit-Aoudia, 2012).

Purpose of the Study

One of the mores of cultural values can be leadership style (Mujtaba & Balboa, 2009; Nguyen & Mujtaba, 2011; Nguyen, Mujtaba, & Ruijs, 2014). In this study, the leadership style of Afghan American nurses was evaluated. The two styles of leadership are relationship-oriented and task-oriented. The reason why the two types of leadership styles are used for comparison is that from an acculturation perspective, Afghans as well as many other cultures have predetermined leadership styles based upon sex which can create

4

personal and organizational obstacles and barriers. For example, Afghan men are conditioned to focus more on tasks and Afghan women are conditioned to focus more on building and maintaining relationships both inside and outside of the house (Aseel, 2003; Aslami, 2011; Hoodfar, 2007).

On the other hand, the US healthcare system is patient centered (Rickert, 2012). Hospitals and medical facilities in America are rated on how well they meet up to the standards of Patient Centered Care (PCC) and are subjected to a multifaceted measurement on how well they meet these standards (Daaleman et al., 2014). Wyatt (2015) and Morrill (2018) emphasized the importance of leaders being relationship oriented in healthcare by focusing on teamwork, trust, mutual respect, and support. Conversely, Kumar and Khiljee (2016) emphasized the importance of leaders being task oriented in healthcare by focusing on efficiency and productivity. Northouse (2004) points out that most researchers are unable to identify the one best leadership style.

Of interest in this proposed research are the variables that predict the task and relationship leadership styles of Afghan American nurses in the US healthcare system. In a study by Fedock and Young (2013), nurse bedside manner was an important factor in hospital rating scores on the HCAPHS survey. Fedock and Young (2013) further expanded on the accountability of nurse managers to complete all tasks and procedures while assuring that nurses were meeting the requirements to take time out and sit and talk to patients and provide an additional element of caring.

Literature gap. An extensive search in a number of databases identified no published works on leadership style of Afghan American nurses working in the US healthcare system. Gap-spotting includes identifying or constructing fairly narrow gaps to more significant gaps. Any gap can enhance the development of existing literature (Colquitt

& Zapata-Phelan, 2007). As a result of the absence of works on the leadership style of Afghan American nurses in the US healthcare system, a descriptive, correlational, quantitative study design was chosen to provide a foundation for future researchers. As Lobo (2005) asserted, descriptive research is foundational for research that is correlational or experimental. Some conception of what X looks like must be known, how it occurs, or where it might be found to theorize about it or test it. Even thoroughly analyzed concepts must be tested for their congruence with reality. Descriptive research begins the process that clarifies what characteristics of a phenomenon or phenomena about amenable to developing theory. Then, other aspects are searched to draw comparisons (correlate) or ways to test (experiment) a theory so that it makes sense in terms of reality. According to Jadalla and Lee (2015), "Culture influences different aspects of life; therefore, cultural differences should not be ignored particularly among recent immigrants whose physical and mental health may be compromised upon immigration and who may be likely to turn to their culture to cope with their transition" (p. 208).

Research Questions

The purpose of the study determines the questions that are asked (White, 2009). The overarching research questions examine acculturation, generation, nursing experience, and sex related to leadership style. In addition, the research questions investigate which variables predict the task-oriented and relationship-oriented leadership styles for Afghan American nurses in the US healthcare system. As such, there are four research questions:

RQ 1. What are the correlations between acculturation, generation, nursing experience, sex, and task-oriented leadership style?

RQ 2. Do acculturation, generation, nursing experience, and sex predict task-oriented leadership?

6

RQ 3. What are the correlations between acculturation, generation, nursing experience, sex, and relationship-oriented leadership style?

RQ 4. Do acculturation, generation, nursing experience, and sex predict relationship-oriented leadership?

Significance of the Study

The significance of the findings shed light on how well Afghan American nurses are prepared for healthcare administrator positions. For example, Afghan American nurses scoring as high task-oriented or high-relationship oriented on the Northouse Leadership Style Questionnaire, might be useful for professional development training depending on the goals of the healthcare facility. Sfantou et al. (2017) explain that leadership style has the potential to have an impact on health-related outcomes.

From a research perspective, this was the first empirical study on Afghan American nurses working in the US healthcare system. Furthermore, there is evidence in the literature that Afghan men are conditioned to focus more on tasks and Afghan women are conditioned to focus more on building and maintaining relationships both inside and outside of the house (Aslami, 2011; Hoodfar, 2007); however, Afghan men are more relationship-oriented (Mujtaba & Sadat, 2010). Lastly, the gap in the research that other researchers have pointed out has to do with future studies comparing specific working populations with similar working backgrounds and demographic variables (Mujtaba, 2010; Mujtaba et al. 2013; Nguyen et al, 2014; Tajaddini et al, 2011; Talwar, 2012; Talwar 2014).

From a practice perspective, the results of this research may assist those Afghan Americans who are able to return to Afghanistan for long or short periods of time to assist with the rebuilding of the war-torn country. The present study assessed the leadership style of Afghan Americans who fall in the *Generation X* and *Generation Y* categories. The reasoning behind this is that most Afghan families who fled Afghanistan in the 1980s came to the US without knowing the American culture or language and dealt with culture shock (i.e., the feeling of disorientation experienced by someone who is suddenly subjected to an unfamiliar culture, way of life, or set of attitudes). Most parents were not in a position to go to school, raise a family, find a stable job to support their family, and learn the language. The children of the baby boomers (Generation X and Generation Y) were able to go to school in the US, learn the language, attain advanced trainings, and focus on their careers (Kaifi, 2010). As highly trained and educated Afghan leaders return to their homeland (i.e., reversing the brain-drain), it becomes imperative for them to be able to provide leadership trainings by providing research and practical examples of how they benefitted from working in the US and being exposed to the American culture. Appendix D contains a letter of support for this research study from Deputy Minister Rohullah Niazi from the Independent Directorate of Local Governance, Government of Islamic Republic of Afghanistan.

In many collectivist cultures and traditions, men are expected to be more task-oriented while women are expected to be more relationship-oriented. If they are, then this can be a potential problem because the US healthcare field expects healthcare professionals to be both task and relationship oriented, and as a result, such clearly defined task or relationship orientations may put at risk the success of the healthcare entity and cause obstacles, barriers, or glass ceilings for Afghan Americans (Snaebjornsson et al., 2015). According to Bombuwela and De Alwis (2013), personal barriers are the most important variables influencing the presence of the glass ceiling, followed by national barriers, cultural barriers, and organizational barriers. Jacobson, Palus, and Bowling (2009) noted that leadership style, behavior, and decision making represent critical components of successful career development and advancement. According to Jones and Jones (2017), with a foundation established regarding the existence of a relationship between leadership style and career success, delving deeper into the how and why questions would provide a significant contribution to the existing body of knowledge. Kumar and Khiljee (2016) explain that clinicians who assume leadership roles need to overcome these barriers and adopt a style of leadership that is inclusive and meets the needs of healthcare professionals. Cultural factors undoubtedly play a role in the effectiveness of any leadership style and national culture could potentially be a predictor of the effectiveness of leadership models in non-Western countries (Vandayani, Kartini, Hilmiana, & Azis, 2015).

Key Terms and Definitions

Acculturation. To assimilate or cause to assimilate a different culture, typically the dominant one. Acculturation occurs when the minority culture changes but is still able to retain unique cultural markers of language, food and customs.

Amalgamate. To join, unite, or merge.

Assertiveness. A culture that values assertiveness.

Assimilation. The process of taking in and fully understanding information or ideas. Assimilation is a process whereby people of a culture learn to adapt to the ways of the majority culture.

Baby boomers. Individuals born in the US between 1946 to 1964.

Brain-drain. The departure of educated or professional people from one country, economic sector, or field for another usually for better pay or living conditions.

Culture shock. The feeling of disorientation experienced by someone who is suddenly subjected to an unfamiliar culture, way of life, or set of attitudes.

Generation X. The group of individuals born between 1965 to 1980.

Generation Y. The group of individuals born after 1980.

Glass ceiling. The phenomenon of unseen, yet unbreakable barrier that keep minorities and women from rising to the upper rungs of the corporate ladder, regardless of their qualifications or achievements.

Hofstede's cultural dimensions. A collection of concepts that include individualism-collectivism, power distance, uncertainty avoidance, masculinity-femininity, and short-term versus long-term orientation.

Humane orientation. A culture that encourages and rewards members for being generous, caring, and altruistic.

Project GLOBE. A project and acronym for Global Leadership and Organizational Behavior Effectiveness that involves a collection of over 150 researchers from over 60 cultures who studied over 17,000 managers in over 900 organizations since 1991 adding more dimensions.

Orientalism. A way of understanding that emphasizes, exaggerates, and distorts differences of Middle Eastern people and cultures as compared to that of Europe and the United States. It often involves seeing Arab culture as exotic, backward, uncivilized, and at times dangerous.

Patriarchy. A term used to refer to autocratic rule by the male head of a family.

Sex egalitarianism. A culture that promotes sex equality.

Transnationalism. A social phenomenon and scholarly research agenda grown out of the heightened interconnectivity between people and the receding economic and social significance of boundaries among nation states.

Chapter II: Literature Review

Chapter II presents the scientific literature on the leadership styles of Afghan American nurses. The focus is on leadership styles that are characterized as relationship-oriented and task-oriented models. Underpinning this study is the proposition that Afghan American nurses in the US healthcare system may or may not have moved away from acculturalization and maintaining their cultural values and, instead, may have become assimilated into the dominant Caucasian American culture. It is speculated that Afghan American nurses working in the US healthcare system may have adopted a relationship leadership style because of the demands on hospitals to engage in a Patient Centered Care (PCC) style of operation (Epstein et al., 2011). In addition, the possibility remains that the Afghan American nurses practice a more dichotomized style of leadership. Three demographic elements will be examined, which include sex, generation identity, and years of nursing experience.

Literature Search Strategy

A literature search was conducted using various database sources to retrieve peer-reviewed and scholarly information on leadership styles of Afghan American nurses. The literature search was performed using university databases that included Alt Health Watch, Health Source, PubMed, EBSCO, Business Source Complete, ProQuest Central, SAGE, and ERIC using several search terms and Boolean operators. Regular internet queries using Internet Explorer and Google Chrome search engines were also conducted. The search terms and Boolean operators included *Afghan leaders* AND *healthcare*, *Afghan* AND *acculturation*, *Afghan* AND *nurses*, *Afghan* AND *Patient Centered Care (PCC)*, *US healthcare* AND *Afghans*, and *Afghan American* AND *leadership style* AND *U.S. healthcare system* (TUI, 2018). Other search strings included *influence* AND *generation*, *sex*, AND *years of nursing experience AND leadership style*, *influence* AND *generation*, *sex*, AND *years of nursing experience AND task-oriented leadership style*, *influence* AND *generation*, *sex*, AND *years of nursing experience AND relationship* OR *people-oriented leadership styles*. Terms related to the desired methodology, design, and analysis were *quantitative*, *comparative*, and *Northouse Leadership Assessment*. The returned research articles were reviewed, assessed for quality, and examined for credibility and applicability with attention to discussions sections and directions for future research.

A comprehensive literature search identified only two empirical studies involving Afghans in the healthcare field, which were conducted in Afghanistan, not in the United States. In general, each study noted the paucity of knowledge in this area and the need for more in depth investigations on leadership values and styles. The first study by Arnold et al. (2014) focused on Afghan healthcare providers in Kabul, Afghanistan. The researchers used a qualitative design, which consisted of 25 semi-structured interviews. According to the authors, this was the first study that focused on Afghan maternity care providers using a qualitative approach to learn more about the culture of care in a Kabul hospital. The results showed that the hospital was overcrowded with care providers struggling to manage the workload, nepotism and cronyism among patients and healthcare providers, lack of accountability among healthcare providers, and being forced into medicine by family members. Female care providers (more relationship-oriented due to cultural norms) were also expected to fulfill their responsibilities at home as mothers, wives, daughters-in-law and entertainers of guests. The authors also mentioned how the care providers were working according to Afghan values as opposed to standardized global biomedical rules and regulations. The study provided deep insight into leadership styles among Afghan healthcare providers and served as a useful model for the current study.

12

The second study conducted by Qarani et al. (2018) examined Afghan nurses in Kabul, Afghanistan. The goal of the research was to explore the educational profile of nursing managers and head nurses at public hospitals using a descriptive, cross-sectional study design. More specifically, a self-administered, pre-tested questionnaire was used to recruit 86 nursing managers and head nurses from 17 public hospitals. The results showed that none of the participants were prepared with higher education in nursing; rather they had only a diploma in nursing; 84.9% of them had completed their nursing diploma before 2002; 11.6% of participants were currently studying; and all were in non-nursing disciplines. On the other hand, all the participants expressed intention for further studies mainly in leadership and management, computer skills, English language, in-service nursing trainings, and higher education in nursing.

The literature search identified several studies that focused on Afghan leadership style, but for those living in Afghanistan, not in the United States. Azizi (2008), the author of a dissertation on Afghan leaders in higher education, traveled to Afghanistan and interviewed educational leaders to learn about their leadership style and what influenced their leadership philosophy. As a result, Azizi (2008) created the *Cultural Exchange Model of Leadership for Afghanistan* with recommendations for a multidimensional leadership style by utilizing: (a) Islamic viewpoints on leadership, (b) cultural considerations regarding leadership, (c) Western styles of leadership, and (d) Eastern viewpoints on leadership. The research also discussed the importance of future research to focus on (a) leadership in the K-12 sector, (b) reasons for the declining leadership roles of women in higher education, and (c) higher education leadership in the provinces of Afghanistan.

Two studies conducted by Talwar (2012, 2014) explored the acculturation experiences in the Afghan immigrant community. In both studies, Talwar (2012, 2014) used a qualitative methodology to interview Afghan immigrants to learn more about

13

acculturation, culture shock, and sex differences. The works did not include considerations about the leadership style or the field of healthcare but provided insights for the current study. Based on the scarcity of research examining the influence of acculturation, assimilation, and this topic in general, a substantial gap in the empirical research literature, regarding Afghan American nurses working in the US healthcare system, was demonstrated.

Historical Background

Most people of the Afghan diaspora in the US have been living there for approximately 20 to 30 years representing several distinct generations (Aslami, 2011; Sadat, 2008). Baby boomers are classified as those who were born in the US between 1946 and 1964. Generation X is classified as those who were born in US between 1965 and 1980, Generation Y is considered those who were born after 1980, and the Z generation is classified as those born in the mid-1990s and early 2000s (Colquitt et al., 2011). It is unlikely that teens and young adults in their early twenties work in healthcare positions prior to obtaining medical training. Children of the baby boomers have strived to obtain an education and are the first generation of Afghan Americans who will be able to contribute to the much-needed literature on Afghan American leadership styles in healthcare. As revealed in the research review, no literature exists in the scientific record related to the leadership orientation of Afghans working in the US healthcare system.

Beginning in the 1930s, different leadership styles were introduced to the field of social science. However, the two main types of leadership styles that are relevant to this research study are task-orientation versus relationship-orientation that has been studied since the 1950s. Northouse (2004) asserts that the leadership style approach focuses the actions but not the substance or identity of leaders.

Starting in the 1950s, a series of studies on leadership styles and behaviors were conducted at Ohio State University and the University of Michigan (Colquitt, Lepine, &

14

Wesson, 2011). The researchers at Ohio State University studied leadership and, as a result, two main leadership style dimensions were discovered: initiating structure and consideration (Fleishman, 1953). Around the same time, similar studies were conducted by the University of Michigan that identified two leadership style dimensions: production-centered (task-oriented) and employee-centered (relations-oriented) (Katz, Maccoby, & Morse, 1950).

Research on Leadership Style

Mujtaba and Alsua (2011) examined the management orientation of working adults and business students in the United States by comparing the leadership perception of 484 respondents from Alaska and Florida regions. The researchers reported that Americans had high scores on both task and relationship orientations but scored a little higher on the relationship-orientation, possibly because of the high emphasis on teamwork and collaboration in universities and the work environment.

Cowsill and Grint (2008) conducted a study that focused on leadership, task, and relationship. The authors discussed the long debate between leadership style and, more specifically, being task or relationship oriented. The study was aimed to evaluate the leadership of the Royal Air Force and the results showed support for both the task and relationship leadership orientations. Cowsill and Grint (2008) asserted that leaders were both focused on the achievement of missions and goals, their relationships with subordinates, and at times the focus was both task oriented and relationship oriented.

Judge et al. (2004) conducted a meta-analysis of the relationship of Ohio State University leadership behaviors entitled *Consideration and Initiating Structure*. The authors concluded that both behaviors were linked to follower motivation and leader effectiveness, with consideration (relationship) being somewhat more important.

Cann and Siegfried (1990) examined the relationship between initiating structure and consideration leadership styles on the one hand and feminine and masculine behaviors on the other. The results showed that consideration is perceived as more feminine and initiating structure is perceived as more masculine. Politis et al. (2018) investigated the relationship between initiating structure and consideration leadership styles, but also creativity and innovation in organizations operating in Arabic and European cultures. The findings of the study revealed that managers with consideration leadership style influenced more positively and significantly the factors of creativity and innovation compared to the managers that exercise initiating structure leadership.

Nursing and Leadership

Over the years, nursing has evolved from a modest caretaker role to a dynamic and challenging profession which requires adaptation to constant change and coordination of personnel, policies, and procedures. Cultural and social awareness is crucial to effective nursing practice. The choices that nurses make in their careers communicate what they value (Blais, 2019). As such, identifying and developing nursing leaders is one of the greatest challenges faced by the nursing profession (Scully, 2015). The concept of leadership is a complex and multi-dimensional phenomenon because there are many definitions and theories of leadership but no universally accepted definitions or theories. However, there is increasing clarity surrounding what true nursing leadership is, and how it differs from management (Grossman & Valiga, 2012).

Nursing leadership includes supporting clinical colleagues and inspiring followers to transform themselves and their situations through development of talents and formation of reciprocal relationships (Caplin-Davies, 2003). One of the most important points to note is that leadership is not necessarily tied to a position of authority (Grossman & Valiga, 2012; Rigoloski, 2013). Due to a lack of authority, the high-usage of teams in healthcare settings, and constant changes in the healthcare industry, nurses can be considered informal leaders who rely upon authentic leading rather than power-wielding tactics available to formal leaders such as managers (Pielstick, 2000).

To navigate the complexities of the modern healthcare environment, bedside nurses must have informal clinical leadership skills to support and empower each other as they make important decisions at the point of care (Rogers, 2017). Transitioning into a professional role as a nurse is challenging. In addition, being able to learn new techniques and perform assigned tasks while getting to know and developing relationships with colleagues can be stressful (Frögéli et al., 2019). Table 1 summarizes the works of Bennis and Nanus (2003) and Grossman and Valiga (2012) to highlight the characteristics and stark differences between leaders and managers.

Table 1

Differences between Leaders and Managers

Concept	Leadership	Management
Position	Selected by a group of followers	*Appointed by someone higher in the organizational hierarchy*
Power base	From knowledge, credibility and ability to motivate followers	*Arising from the position of authority*
Goals/vision	Arise from personal interests and passion, may not be synonymous with organizational goals	*Prescribed by the organization*

Concept	Leadership	Management
Innovative ideas	Developed, tested, and encouraged among all group members	*Allowed provided they do not interfere with task accomplishment*
Risk level	High risk, creativity and innovation are involved	*Low risk, balance and maintaining status quo*
Degree of order	Relative disorder seems to be created	*Rational and controlled*
Nature of activities	Related to vision and judgment	*Related to efficiency and cost effectiveness*
Focus	People	*Systems and structure*
Perspective	Long range with an eye on the horizon	*Short range with an eye on the bottom line*
Degree of Freedom	Freestanding, not limited to organizational position of authority	*Tied to designated position within the organization*
Actions	"Does the right thing"	*"Does things right"*

In the past, healthcare organizations appointed formal visionary leaders to address organizational challenges and cope with the complexities of modern healthcare (Downey, Parslow, & Smart, 2011). Yet, at a time when healthcare organizations and clinicians need to increase their ability to adapt to complexity and continuous change for safety, quality, and efficiency, hierarchical healthcare leadership structures were flattened (Rogers, 2017). The trend to streamline the formal leadership structure and reduce overhead expenses has the net effect of increasing administrative and managerial responsibilities assigned to nurse managers and first-line supervisors (Downey et al., 2011).

Informal clinical leadership is a valuable resource for helping direct care nurses adapt to the ever-changing and sometimes uncertain environment of modern healthcare (Downey et al., 2011; Fardellone et al., 2014; Larsson & Sahlsten, 2016). Becoming an informal leader stretches the comfort zone of nurses in a number of ways (Ross, 2014). For example, as informal leaders push themselves in a leadership position, they will learn about their own strengths and weaknesses and how they can better lead others. As such, this valuable information can be impactful to the future careers of nurses and can potentially provide more formal opportunities and career advancement. Conceptually, informal clinical leadership is known to be practiced by nurses at the point of care (AACN, 2008; Downey et al., 2011; IOM, 2010; Mannix et al., 2013; NHSLA, 2013). Bedside nurses are positioned at the point of care to make critical contributions by coordinating complex care, promoting patient safety, and reducing medication errors and infection rates, while ensuring safe patient transition throughout healthcare systems (IOM, 2010).

The complex modern healthcare environment is full of challenges to providing safe, high quality, and effective care. Nurses at all practice levels are called to lead the charge to address these challenges (IOM, 2010). Healthcare leadership research has predominantly focused on the attributes and behavior of managers or other leaders with formal authority, which fails to distinguish the unique leadership behavior and contributions of clinicians at the point of care (Downey et al., 2011; Howieson & Thiagarajah, 2011; Mannix, Wilkes, & Daly, 2013). According to Grimm (2010), nurses are leaders by nature of the profession. Regardless of their level of practice or setting, nurses frequently are called upon to make decisions and act in ways that can profoundly change the outcomes of their patients and the organization of which they are a part. Different circumstances require different qualities, traits, and styles. Task-centered, sometimes referred to as functional, nursing is conceived as a narrow, specialist approach to care delivery. Patient-centered nursing views tasks as best delivered in an integrated and holistic way that includes tailored care to meet individual needs (Kessler et al., 2015).

Leadership Style and Sex

Sex was a particularly important aspect of this dissertation research since the Afghan culture has pre-determined roles for both sexes. As Aseel (2003) explains, "Traditionally, men were the breadwinners and women were the caretakers" (p. 4). Afghan men are conditioned to focus more on tasks and Afghan women are conditioned to focus more on building and maintaining relationships both inside and outside of the household (Aseel, 2003; Aslami, 2011; Hoodfar, 2007). Asking critical questions about sex, most often, leads to the discovery of positive outcomes, as well as unintended consequences. The results of such inquiries have the potential to improve reduce sex inequities (Tannenbaum et al., 2016).

Zoppi (2004) examined the relationship between self-perceived leadership, acculturation, and individualistic or collectivistic behaviors in Latino women leaders using the Acculturation Rating Scale for Mexican Americans-II (ARSMA-II). The investigator recommended the need for additional research targeting sex differences in leadership and acculturation. Trevino (2010) conducted a similar study on acculturation and leadership styles but focused on elected Latino leaders. The purpose of this exploratory study was to examine the scores of elected Latino leaders tested on an acculturation and leadership scale. The author noted that the absence of sex in the study could be attributed to the lack of a single probing question on sex within the current research surveys that were utilized.

Nguyen, Mujtaba, and Ruijs (2014) conducted a study that focused on the task and relationship orientations of a Dutch sample ($n = 208$), which included sex differences as well. Dutch females scored higher on the both the task oriented and the relationship-oriented leadership styles when compared to their male counterparts. One of the main findings of this study was that overall, the Dutch, regardless of sex, depend more on a relationship-oriented leadership style.

Mujtaba and Balboa (2009) conducted a study that focused on the task and relationship orientations of a Filipino sample ($n = 192$). The Filipino respondents may be focusing more on their relationship orientation because of their high-context and collective culture. When comparing the task scores of Filipinos to Americans, the results of the study show that Filipino respondent task scores were significantly lower than those of American respondents. Furthermore, male and female respondents in the Philippines had similar scores on both task and relationship orientations.

Nguyen, Ermasova, Geyfman, and Mujtaba (2015) conducted a study on the task and relationship orientations of a Russian sample ($n = 519$). Results show that Russians are more relationship-oriented, however, the government sector prefers individuals who are highly task-oriented. Furthermore, the authors mention that older Russians tend to be more task-oriented when compared to the younger groups and Russian males are more task oriented when compared to Russian females. Table 2 lists previous research studies that focused on task and relationship leadership styles of different ethnic groups.

Table 2

Comparable Studies

Authors (Year)	Ethnicity (Sample Size)	Results
Mujtaba, B. G., & Balboa, A. (2009).	Filipino ($n = 192$)	Relationship orientation falls in the "high" range and task orientation in the "moderately high" range.
Mujtaba, B.G., & Sadat, S.K. (2010).	Afghan ($n = 106$)	Different scores on task and relationship orientations.

Mujtaba, B. G., & Alsua, C. J. (2011).	American ($n = 484$)	Scores for task and relationship fall into the high range but slightly higher relationship scores.
Mujtaba, B.G., Khanfar, N. M., & Khanfar, S. M. (2010).	Oman ($n = 129$)	Task orientation falls into the high range and relationship orientation into the high range.
Mujtaba, B. G., Cai, Hongman, Lian, Y., & Ping, H. (2013).	Chinese ($n = 381$)	Significantly higher scores on relationship orientation compared to task orientation.
Nguyen, L. D., Mujtaba, B. G., & Ruijs, A. (2014).	Dutch ($n = 208$)	Men seem to be less task-oriented and less relationship-oriented compared to women.
Manyak, T., & Mujtaba, B.G. (2013).	Ugandan ($n = 139$)	High relationship-orientation and task-orientations.
Nguyen, L. D., & Mujtaba, B. G. (2011).	Vietnamese ($n = 188$)	Moderately high scores on both the relationship and task orientations.
Nguyen, L. D., Ermasova, N., Geyfman, V., & Mujtaba, B.G. (2015).	Russian ($n = 519$)	Older subjects tend to be more task-oriented when compared to the younger subjects and males more task oriented when compared to females.
Begum, R. & Mujtaba, B. (2016).	Pakistani ($n = 380$)	Managers seem to use both styles in moderation. While they are more relationships focused, they demonstrate an overall balance between the two styles.

Leadership and Generational Affiliation

Generational affiliation is of particular importance to this dissertation thesis because Afghan American baby boomers were not included in the study. Most baby boomers were unable to obtain a formal education in the US when they were forced to escape Afghanistan during the Soviet invasion from 1979 to 1989 due to language barriers (Stempel et al., 2017). As such, the progenies of the baby boomers will be studied. Aseel (2003) explains, "Career advancement was a distant goal, and became something that [Afghan] parents eventually wished for their children rather than for themselves" (p. 29). More specifically, Afghan American nurses who fall in the Generation X (born between 1965 to 1980) and Generation Y (born after 1980) groups were the two groups of focus for the present study. Aghamirza (2015) examined the acculturation levels and experiences of first-generation immigrant

22

leaders at the district offices and school sites in the Mid-Atlantic region of the United States. The recommendation for future researchers of acculturation was to focus on the age of immigrants upon arrival to the United States and levels of their education before and after immigration. Aghamirza also suggested evaluating familiarity with the English language before and after immigration. Lastly, Aghamirza endorsed the conduct of narrative or ethnographic studies to gain a deeper understanding of knowledge and experiences of first-generation immigrant leaders.

One major distinction, between Afghan Americans who fall in the Generation X category when compared to Generation Y category, is that the Generation X group were born in Afghanistan and the Generation Y group were born outside of Afghanistan. Consequently, evaluating age or generational affiliation is important for the purpose of this study.

Work Experience and Leadership Style

In the past, it was normal for many employees to stay with an organization for their entire career (Hall, 2002). As of 2020, employees change jobs more rapidly than before. For example, one report estimated that the population born between 1957 and 1964 changed jobs on average 11.7 times throughout their career (McKay, 2018). According to Doyle (2018), many workers spend five years or fewer in every job over their vocation.

Work experience is the amount of job-related experience an individual has accumulated over the course of their career (Quinones, Ford, & Teachout 1995; Tesluk & Jacobs, 1998). Other researchers believe that work experience is most often conceptualized in quantitative terms (e.g., job tenure) that reflect either the time or amount of experience (Tesluk & Jacobs, 1998). The accumulation of work experience is more likely to influence cognitive and affective reactions to the workplace (Forteza & Prieto, 1994). Work experience has the potential to influence how an employee performs at work by focusing more on relationships than tasks or vice versa.

A number of researchers have suggested using work experience (i.e., less than five years or greater than five years) as a variable to see how work experience influences the scores on the Leadership Style Questionnaire (Mujtaba, 2010; Mujtaba & Isomura, 2011; Tajaddini & Mujtaba, 2010). In the healthcare field, it is common for seasoned employees within an organization to be promoted to leadership positions because they are already acclimated with the employees, culture, and goals of the organization. According to the Bureau of Labor Statistics (2018), an individual who would like to become a medical or health services manager needs to have a bachelor's degree and approximately five years of work experience.

Leadership and Acculturation

There have been several studies conducted on leadership and acculturation. Zoppi (2004) examined the relationship of self-perceived leadership, acculturation, and individualistic versus collectivistic behaviors in female Latino leaders using the Acculturation Rating Scale for Mexican Americans-II (ARSMA-II). The study used a quantitative, descriptive, and exploratory research approach to answer the research questions. One finding was that transformational leadership behaviors were significantly related to collectivism factors, whereas transactional leadership behaviors were significantly related to individualistic factors. The author mentioned that additional research should target sex differences in leadership and acculturation, including individualism versus collectivism styles.

A mixed-methods study by Iron Cloud (2019) on the Oglala Lakota people of the Pine Ridge Indian Reservation found that the participants found themselves in a time of rapid change, a time of biculturalism and multiculturalism. One of the primary questions of this study focused on whether acculturation predicts leadership styles. The levels of acculturation were low, traditional (17.6%), moderate, bicultural (68.6%) and high, assimilated (13.7%). Qualitative themes revealed leadership values similar to servant leadership among all six respondents regardless of acculturation level.

Trevino (2010) conducted a study on acculturation and leadership styles of elected Latino leaders. The purpose of this exploratory study was to examine how a group of elected Latino leaders scored on an acculturation and leadership scale. The study also provided an understanding of how elected Latino leaders define and experience leadership based on their acculturation level and leadership styles. Trevino (2010) defined acculturation levels as individuals progressing through the process of socialization changes in thinking about their values and traditions. The stages each individual goes through represent levels of adaptation to the dominant society often involving religious practices, diet, healthcare and social institutions. The results of the study also add to the current body of literature on Latino leadership because the findings confirmed an association between acculturation level and leadership style. The author pointed out that the absence of sex in the study was attributed to the lack of a single probing question on sex within the current research surveys utilized.

Paris (2003) conducted a study on acculturation, assimilation, leadership styles and its consequences on job satisfaction. The study examined the consequences of culture for job satisfaction of six cultural groups in the Honolulu Fire Department (HFD). Results of the study indicated that the six cultural groups (American, Chinese, Filipino, Japanese, Part-Hawaiian, and "others") of the Honolulu Fire Department showed evidence of assimilation. Upon comparison of cultural group scores with corresponding Motherland scores, most HFD cultural groups were shown to have retained very little remnants of culture from their Motherland. The overall results indicated that most groups were satisfied with job location and physical working conditions, but were less satisfied with personal growth and the least satisfied with leadership styles and earnings.

Afghan Leadership Style

For the past century, the topic of leadership style and leader-follower relationships has been investigated by a number of scholars. Many scholars have questioned what the most effective method is for leading others. A leadership style is a consistent behavior that is exercised in a number of predicaments. As such, the two main types of leadership styles that are relevant to this dissertation research are the task-oriented and relationship-oriented.

As mentioned previously, the work of Mujtaba and Sadat (2010) focused on the task and leadership orientation of Afghans living in Afghanistan (i.e., locals) and Afghan expatriates. The total number of local Afghan participants was 106 (Males, $n = 84$; Females, $n = 22$) and the total number of expatriates was 219 (Males, $n = 123$; Females, $n = 96$). The expatriate respondents were mostly working adults living in the United States but working in Afghanistan. The study used two versions of a questionnaire. One version was in English and the other version was translated into Dari, the dominant language of Afghanistan. The Dari version was distributed to individuals working in Herat, Afghanistan. Overall, the results showed that local males and females had similar "high" scores on both task and relationship orientations. However, expatriate males and females who were mostly adults living in the US scored differently on the questionnaire. Expatriate males had "high" scores for both task and relationship orientations, whereas expatriate females had moderately high scores for task orientation and high scores for relationship orientation. A major study limitation worth noting was the small sample size of Afghan female locals ($n = 22$). Furthermore, the city of Herat in Afghanistan borders Iran, and as a result, is highly influenced by its more industrialized, sophisticated, and developed neighbor. For example,

26

Iran has a literacy of 77%, life expectancy of 70.56 years, and an infant mortality rate of 39.3 per 1,000 live births, whereas Afghanistan has a literacy of 28.1%, life expectancy of 43.77 years, and an infant mortality rate of 160.2 per 1,000 live births (Weatherby et al., 2009). It may be that Iranian leadership style is influenced by Western principles which have been carried over to the city of Herat, Afghanistan (Kumar & Rehnamol, 2017).

Azizi (2008) conducted a study on leaders of higher education in Afghanistan that consisted of interviewing seven male leaders in higher education and seven female leaders in parliament. The author explained the importance of Afghan leaders using leadership styles that will instigate the overall scheme of a powerful nation building. As a result of his research, Azizi (2008), developed the Cultural Exchange Model of Leadership for Afghanistan which encompasses Eastern viewpoints on literature, Islamic viewpoints on leadership, Western styles of leadership, and cultural considerations regarding leadership.

Mujtaba and Kaifi (2010) conducted a study on the transformational leadership style of Afghans ($n = 300$) and Americans ($n = 502$). The researchers concluded that female American respondents had a significantly higher transformational leadership orientation than their Afghan female colleagues. Younger Afghans had a significantly higher tendency toward a transformational leadership orientation than their American counterparts. Moreover, Mujtaba and Kaifi (2010) also conducted a study on the leadership orientation of working adults in Afghanistan ($n = 219$) compared to the US ($n = 87$). The small number of American females ($n = 31$) and the survey not being translated to the native language of Afghanistan were both major limitations of the study. However, one main result showed that Afghan females had significantly lower tasks scores when compared to their relationship scores.

A study by Rahmani (2016) investigated political leadership in Afghanistan. The author pointed out that political leadership and the actual characteristics of an Afghan leader

27

have never been studied. According to the Rahmani (2016) study, some of the most important attributes of a good leader are being educated, having morals and values, and being a devout Muslim. The researcher also explained how different ethnic groups within Afghanistan had a different definition for what a leader is. For example, Pashtuns associate the word *elder* to leadership while Tajiks associate the word *guide* to leadership.

American Leadership Style

In the US, effective leaders are expected to be able to focus on tasks while maintaining and developing relationships at the same time. Both leadership orientations are important, and, in some cases, it may be more beneficial to focus more on tasks than relationships or vice versa. In other cases, depending on the industry, leaders could be high in one orientation or a balance on both orientations (Blake & Mouton 1966; Mujtaba et al., 2010; Nguyen et al., 2014; Schermerhorn et al., 2008). According to Sherwood and DePaolo (2005), the task context includes how a manager will complete tasks with and through people which has to do with planning, organizing, leading, and controlling. The authors further explained that the relationship context involves showing concern for subordinates, providing unconditional emotional support, and open communication.

Several researchers have discussed the task versus relationship dichotomy and recommended leaders to be both task and relationship oriented. For example, Begum and Mujtaba (2016) discussed how leaders should be flexible to accommodate the contextual demands in their leadership style to maintain a healthy balance of task and relationship orientation. Mujtaba et al. (2010) explained the importance of having a balance in order for organizational goals to be accomplished. Cowsill and Grint (2008) discussed how leaders who over-focus on building relationships without a purpose or over-focus on task completion are unlikely to succeed in the long run. Kavanaugh (1986) noted that the combination of task and relationship orientations have the capacity to unify teams and influence leader effectiveness.

Task-Oriented and Relationship-Oriented Leadership Styles in US Healthcare

According to Cascardo (2016), times have changed what is expected of a leader in healthcare. For example, in the past, hospitals hired leaders who had a high task orientation with strong clinical skills, focus on high patient volume, and were suitable to fulfill the role of chief medical officer. Task orientated care is a model of delegating nurses to patient care with a focus on the task rather than the patient (Fallon et al., 2018). In addition to focusing on patient engagement, focus should be broadened to include relationships among all staff. If the employees are not working together effectively, this may interfere with establishment of positive staff–patient relationships (Kiwanuka et al., 2019). Currently in 2020, there is a need for physician leaders with a balanced leadership style and exceptional people skills (i.e., relationship orientation) that are able to communicate, build trust, and commitment among employees to accomplish organizational goals (i.e., task orientation). Students learn and use a servant leadership style during nursing school and as they develop in their professional nursing role (Anderson, 2016). Furthermore, the Healthcare Leadership Alliance (HLA) competency model emphasizes five competency domains of which three domains are dedicated to soft skills such as communication, leadership, and professionalism (Stefl, 2008). Delmatoff and Lazarus (2014) discussed the importance of healthcare leaders to have a high relationship orientation where the individual is able to mask their true feelings to avoid conflict or confrontation and are sensitive to the needs of other people, which is expected of why they chose a career in healthcare.

Kilpatrick (2009) noted that the effectiveness of health organizations is affected by the relationships formed by people, technology, resources and administration in providing health care. Grandy and Holton (2013) described healthcare leadership as a process that focuses on relationships by building and maintaining relationships, motivating others while also considering operational and strategic initiatives. Morley (2018) mentioned that two studies in the *International Journal of Nursing Studies* found that leaders operating in a manner consistent with the relationship-oriented theory of leadership were more effective than their task-oriented counterparts (Coomber & Barriball, 2007; Smith, Profetto-McGrath, & Cummings, 2009). However, the research also indicated that leaders who practiced elements of both theories were the most effective. According to the University of Central Michigan, there is growing evidence that both initiating structure and consideration are important for successfully leading teams. Furthermore, Judge et al. (2004) concluded both consideration and initiating structure had important outcomes on a number of criteria that most would argue were important indicators of effective leadership. The authors asserted that consideration and structure have virtually disappeared in contemporary research; therefore, these concepts should be integrated with more recent theorizing in leadership research.

The US healthcare field is very diverse, both from the provider and the consumer point of view. The success of patient care models and administrative functions depend on the professionalism and leadership style of the healthcare leaders. According to Kumar and Khiljee (2015), there are nine components of an effective healthcare leader that mainly focus on relationship and task skills:

1. *Leading with care.* Recognizing the needs and behaviors of the team with mutual support for each other, enabling the spread of a caring environment beyond the team's area.
2. *Sharing the vision.* Communicating with credibility and trust, having a clear direction for long-term goals and inspiring confidence for the future.
3. *Engaging the team.* Trusting in the team and supporting creative participation.

4. *Influencing for results.* Engaging with and adapting to others, to develop a collaborative approach to working and to build sustainable commitments.

5. *Evaluating information.* Sourcing information from a wide area and thinking creatively to develop new concepts.

6. *Inspiring shared purpose.* Whilst adhering to principles and values, taking personal risks and making courageous challenges for the benefit of the service.

7. *Connecting our service.* Reflecting on how different parts of the system relate to one another, understanding the politics of the organization, and adopting outside approaches that work well.

8. *Developing capability.* Providing opportunities for individuals and teams to develop, enabling improved longer-term capabilities.

9. *Holding to account.* Having clear expectations, challenging for continuous improvement and creating a mindset for innovative change.

The US healthcare system depends more and more on teams, technology, and a culture of adaptability. Collaborative efforts and engagement of local trainers and teams can improve health care quality and outcomes (Hosey et al., 2016).

Many healthcare organizations include globalization in their strategic tactics. The team approach to treating patients is essential for international market infiltration. The team approach to treating patients is also being used between the US and the United Arab Emirates (UAE). For example, according to Trade Arabia (2018), the Ras Al Khaimah (RAK)-based Arabian Healthcare Group formed a strategic alliance with Dignity Health which is based in the United States. The alliance will depend heavily on telemedicine, which can assist with second opinion programs, consultations, and patient e-visits. Arabian Healthcare Group physicians will work collectively with American physicians to provide exceptional quality care for an affordable price. Therefore, new technological advancements support strong relationships among nurses and patients and changes delegation of tasks among nurses and doctors. The division of labor gives more responsibility and professional discretion for nurses (Christian & Nickelsen, 2019).

According to Mhoon-Walker (2013), executive leaders and subordinates are facing innovative challenges due to intensified concentration on healthcare accountability. Strategic leaders in healthcare have the ability to formulate and implement organizational changes that will provide competitive advantages for the organization. Understanding leadership and implementing an effective leadership style in any industry can be challenging. Afghan professionals working in the US healthcare sector may have a unique leadership style based upon their Eastern-Western backgrounds.

Previous Research on Leadership Style in Healthcare

Many researchers have inquired about the optimum leadership style in healthcare because the literature has identified the importance of leadership style on patient outcomes, organizational culture, and also because the industry is undergoing a major paradigm shift (going from volume to value), which has been driven by the recent healthcare reforms that were initiated by the PPACA (the Patient Protection and Affordable Care Act). According to Sfantou et al. (2017), there is evidence that leadership style is a key element for quality of healthcare and, more specifically, effective leadership is among the most critical components that lead an organization to effective and successful outcomes. Therefore, the question becomes, which leadership style is the most effective in healthcare? There are several styles of leadership, while six types appear to be more common during the time of this study: transformational, transactional, autocratic, laissez-faire, task-oriented, and relationship-oriented leadership (Sfantou et al., 2017). As such, healthcare leaders are needed to help motivate, support, influence, and possibly change the way healthcare professionals understand and perform their jobs.

It is important to mention that effective leadership encompasses a high-quality work environment leading to a positive safety climate that assures favorable patient outcomes because failure of leadership to create a quality workplace can harm patients (Sfantou et al., 2017). Leadership styles play a pivotal role in enhancing quality measure in healthcare. Barnes (2016) discussed one key finding of how transformational leaders were able to motivate and lead staff effectively, which implies that transformational leadership styles have the potential for improving organizational change processes since human needs are considered. The result may explain why healthcare organizations believe that leadership training is needed for all employees and not only formal leaders. According to Edmonstone (2017), in order for healthcare employees to allow staff the opportunity to participate in leadership development programs, there needs to be a significant return-on-investment on their future personal and organizational performance. With all the ongoing changes in healthcare, researchers have considered the relationship between transformational leadership and happiness at work. The focus may explain why Wheatley (2010) noted a transformational leader was needed to lead healthcare organizations through 21st-century challenges. A transactional leadership style can be beneficial in healthcare. Barnes (2016) explained that both transformational and transactional leaders stated that they engaged in positive talk with their staff. Bullock (2015) stated that transactional leaders first try to understand the task that needs to be accomplished and then proceed to set-up an exchange with the follower through a mutual agreement. Leadership studies conducted in other industries revealed that men rated higher as transactional leaders and women rated higher as transformational leaders (Bass & Riggio, 2006; Carless, 1998; Lantz & Maryland, 2008; Pounder & Coleman, 2002). A servant leadership style can be effective for leading healthcare organizations because of the nurturing style that is needed to help improve patient outcomes. According to Negron (2012), servant leadership is a style in which individuals choose to be servant primarily and leader secondarily. However, after using an interpretive biography methodology, Negron (2012) concluded that even though servant leaders contribute greatly to employee development, this particular leadership style may fail to motivate the employees to accomplish the organizational goals. As noted above, researchers have experienced difficulty in identifying one best style of leadership for all settings and organizations (Northouse, 2004).

Theoretical Orientation and Conceptual Framework

Acculturation theory. The notion of acculturation originated from the fields of anthropology and sociology of the 20th century (Park & Burgess, 1921; Redfield, Linton & Herskovits, 1936). Acculturation theory has been used to better understand the dynamics of people from diverse cultural backgrounds amalgamating into other cultures. Acculturation occurs when individuals adopt the attitudes, values, customs, beliefs, and behaviors of another culture (Abraido-Lanza et al., 2006). According to Oudenhoven and Ward (2013), acculturation refers to the changes arising from intercultural contact. Marin and Marin (1991) found the process of learning and behaviorally adapting to a new culture is labeled acculturation. Acculturation is the process that involves mutual changes that occur when two or more cultural groups encounter one another. As such, most Afghan Americans have lived in the US for at least 20 to 30 years and, as a result, may have been influenced by the dominant culture. The acculturation process has four stages: (a) *honeymoon* or Assimilation phase, (b) *culture shock* or Separation phase, (c) *gradual adjustment* or Marginalization phase, and (d) *feeling at home* or Integration phase. According to Oudenhoven and Ward (2013), although transnationalism may reflect international linkages across several countries,

34

in most cases, the term is used to refer to bilateral transnationalism, which is the process by which immigrants maintain multiple social relations between their societies of origin and settlement.

Previous research on acculturation. Ndika (2013) conducted a study on first-generation Nigerian immigrants ($n = 104$) in the United States. The report noted, "Most of the Nigerian participants, who had resided in the United States for more than 20 years ($n = 33$), might have developed complex strategies with which they adapt to the American lifestyle" (p. 5). Moreover, the majority of the participants stated that they used a combination of assimilation or separation acculturation strategies to adapt to the mainstream US culture. Kheirkhah (2003) conducted a qualitative study on adaptation patterns among Iranian immigrants ($n = 17$) in the US who were forced to leave Iran due to the 1979 Revolution. The findings of this study include "two prominent acculturation strategies: (a) segregation or separation of public and private lives in order to preserve the home culture, on the one hand, and (b) integration of private and public lives in order to acculturate, on the other" (p. 25). Another finding was the presence of the Iranian community in the US which aided adaptation of the participants. Further research by Deguchi (2006) examined acculturation patterns of Japanese women ($n = 10$) in America. The women in the study entered the US between 1948 and 1977 and lived in the US for an average of 39.2 years. Some reasons why the women moved to the US was because of marrying an American, job transfer of their Japanese husbands, or study abroad programs. The author discussed being "bicultural—ways of relating to the dominant culture and the culture of origin" (p. 191). Four acculturation experiences emerged from the narratives: (a) Japanese women who successfully acculturated to the mainstream American society, (b) Japanese women who did not fit in their own Japanese culture, (c) Japanese women who embraced being Japanese and

Japanese-American, and (d) Japanese women who considered themselves a guest in the American society.

Afghans and acculturation. Frogel (2016) conducted a study that examined Afghan Jews, their children, and the psychological impact of acculturation on the first and second generations. More specifically, the author used a phenomenological qualitative approach and focused on the influence of acculturation on Afghan Jews living throughout the United States. There were 12 participants interviewed for the study. Results indicated that Afghan Jews experienced similar acculturation processes as several other immigrant populations in the US and endorsed the acculturation strategies of traditionality, assimilation, and integration.

Stempel et al. (2016) conducted a study on Afghan Americans living in Northern California to learn more about the stress of immigration, adaptation, and acculturation. There were 259 participants in this quantitative study and the researchers used a 24-item Talbieh Brief Distress Inventory (TBDI) as a general measure of distress among immigrants. The survey was translated to Dari for non-English speakers. The four significant factors that emerged from this study were: (a) Afghan women stressed more about family ties when compared to their male counterparts, (b) Afghan men stressed more about speaking and understanding English when compared to their female counterparts, (c) Afghan traditional-oriented women and open-minded men had lower levels of stress, and (d) Afghan males stressed more about acculturation when compared to their female counterparts. Moreover, Stempel et al. (2016) reported that sex "moderated the effects of four factors on levels of distress" (p. 1). Throughout the article, the authors discussed the refugee experience when resettling in a developed country and having to deal with depression, anxiety, and post-traumatic stress disorder (PTSD).

Abbasi-Shavazi and Sadeghi (2015) conducted a study on the "socio-cultural adaptation of second-generation Afghans in Iran" (p. 96). Due to many years of war and civil war in Afghanistan, several Afghans migrated and created transnational networks with neighboring countries such as Iran, Pakistan, and India. The authors examined how second-generation Afghans adapted to the host society and to what extent their adaptation patterns correlated with demographic and contextual factors. After gathering the data from the Afghans Adaptation Survey and analyzing the data using multivariate analysis, the results revealed that second-generation Afghans had a variety of adaptation patterns. According to Abbasi-Shavazi and Sadeghi (2015), "integration is the most prevalent pattern of adaptation and acculturation (which is observed among 35.8 percent of respondents) followed by separation (33.3%), assimilation (17.1%) and marginalization (13.8%)" (p. 89). Furthermore, it is important to note that socio-demographic factors such as sex, education, ethnicity, perceived discrimination, family context, neighborhood characteristics, and length and city of residence were associated with the Afghan adaptation patterns.

Talwar (2014) conducted a qualitative study on acculturation of Afghans who migrated to the United States. The sample consisted of 17 Afghan immigrants who fled Afghanistan after the Soviet invasion of Afghanistan. Talwar explained how there are very few studies that have explored the acculturation experiences in the Afghan immigrant community. The results of this study showed that the Afghan acculturation process revealed an awareness of the wide gap between the Afghan and US culture and an effort to reconcile the disparities between both cultures (p. 178).

Talwar (2012) conducted a qualitative study on Afghan refugees in the US and, more specifically, analyzed the experiences of seven Afghan males that migrated to the United States. The Afghan men in this sample "shared experiences of cultural bereavement, a sense of loss for their country of origin, stressors related to status loss, all of which could serve as useful variables for mental health research and potential intervention in the future" (pp. 134-135). The findings of this study also showed the culture and sex role differences of which immigrant men adapt in the country of migration.

Kaifi (2009) conducted a qualitative study on Afghan American leaders in the post September 11th (9/11) era. Kaifi explained how Afghan American leaders were emerging in all fields. There were Afghan Americans who are police officers, lawyers, medical doctors, professors, and business owners. First generation Afghan Americans worked hard to become respectable leaders in all fields. One of the participants mentioned that she found herself in between two cultures: Afghan culture and the Western culture. The results of the study showed that the Afghan identity is endangered in the West, and can become extinct because of segregation, alienation, isolation, and discrimination. As such, Afghan leaders changed their names, identities, and traditions to be accepted in this society. One case in point was Dr. Mohammad Humayon Qayoumi (former President of San Jose State University from 2011 to 2015 and California State University, East Bay from 2006 to 2011) who would go by the name, "Mo" (Jennings, 2015). Kaifi (2010) also interviewed an Afghan American girl who was confused about her identity in her younger years that explained how growing up in the diaspora of an immigrant family, she found herself confused about her identity whether she was an Afghan or an American. Aseel (2003) explained that Afghan Americans were often put difficult positions of leading Afghan lifestyles while home with parents simultaneously leading Western lifestyles outside the home to fit in with mainstream society.

Previous research on cultural dimensions. According to Lo et al. (2017), the introduction of Hofstede's dimensions of culture allowed for cross-cultural analyses of organizations in new, unprecedented ways. Hofstede's contributions remain the dominant cultural theory applied in administrative research. Through the analysis of organization postings of the "About Us" self-description and visual representation, the purpose of the research was to determine how well Hofstede's cultural dimensions applied to a virtual culture on Facebook as used by Global 500 corporations. Germanic Europe was least likely to represent the power distance indicator, and Southern Asian and Germanic Europe clusters were more likely to show elements of short-term orientations. Both Latin America and Latin Europe clusters were more likely to demonstrate characteristics of uncertainty avoidance while the Anglo, Nordic Europe, and Oceanic clusters were more likely to reflect the masculine-feminine divide.

Khlif (2016) used the Hofstede cultural dimensions in accounting research. Results showed that individualism was generally a significant positive effect on corporate reporting policy, while it had a significant negative effect on tax evasion. High levels of masculinity were generally related to low disclosure environments and aggressive accounting manipulations. Finally, long-term orientation was investigated in connection with social environmental disclosure, and empirical findings suggested that such a cultural dimension is associated with increased social and environmental reporting practices.

Al Anezi and Al Ansari (2016) investigated the sex differences of the Hofstede cultural dimensions in a sample of Kuwaiti participants. Statistical analysis utilized independent sample t-tests to examine the sex differences among the Hofstede dimensions of national culture. The results revealed significant sex differences: males obtained a higher score than females on individualism and masculinity, and females obtained a higher score than males on power distance and long-term orientation.

The study by Hur et al. (2015) provided brand managers with empirical support for which brand-related activities are likely to be most effective in country markets distinguished by their cultural differences. Importantly, global firms should be careful when attempting to enhance the long-term customer-brand relationship and global brand values must be communicated for each culture appropriately. The results provided brand management guidelines for global brand or marketing managers who attempt to enter India (individualism, reduced long-term orientation, femininity) and China (collectivism, long-term orientation, masculinity).

Cronje (2011) used the Hofstede cultural dimensions to interpret cross-cultural blended teaching and learning. According to the author, the Hofstede dimension of power distance explained the lack of self-confidence among students and the fact the students had difficulty taking initiative, preferring to let the apparently more powerful professor take the responsibility. The issue was compounded by high levels of uncertainty avoidance, which could explain why students required much guidance in terms of requirements and assessment rubrics, and why the student products were very similar in the early stages of the program. On the other hand, the constant challenge that the professors made to the students to take initiative and to take risks led students to rely on one another, which was unexpected in a highly individualist cultural context.

Afghans and cultural dimensions. From an orientalist view, the Afghan culture is unique and complex. Traditionally, Afghan culture has always influenced the ways that society functions in Afghanistan. There are two most important core beliefs of Afghan culture: pride (*namoos*) and honor (*nang*). To illustrate these core beliefs, pride and honor were recently highlighted in a biographical Hollywood movie titled, *Lone Survivor*, where an Afghan family protected and assisted a US Navy SEAL who was hunted by the Taliban (Lone Survivor, 2013). The Afghan family could have easily handed over the injured US soldier to the Taliban but because of pride and honor they provided the US soldier (their respected guest) with food, shelter, and defended him against the Taliban. Table 3 (adapted from Colquitt et al., 2011; Mujtaba, 2013) details the differences in Hofstede dimensions between Afghan and American cultures.

Table 3 shows that Americans and Afghans have similar cultural values in some areas and different cultural values in other areas. In terms of cultural dimensions, the general culture of Afghanistan is likely to be low on individualism, high on power distance, masculinity, and uncertainty avoidance, and short-term oriented (Mujtaba, 2013).

Table 3

Hofstede's Dimensions in the United States and Afghanistan

Dimensions	United States	Afghanistan
Individualistic vs. collectivist	Individualistic	Collectivistic
Power distance	Low	High
Uncertainty avoidance	Low	High
Masculinity-femininity	Masculinity	Masculinity
Short-term vs. long-term orientation	Short-term	Short-term

Theoretical framework. The first theme that emerged from the literature was the leadership dichotomy of task or relationship orientation. Leadership, and the study of it, has roots in the beginning of civilization. Egyptian rulers, Greek heroes, and religious patriarchs all have one concept in common regarding leadership (Wren, 1995). According to Nguyen et al. (2014), many leadership models in the behavioral approach differentiate behavioral patterns, or leadership styles. A leadership style is a pattern of behavior that leaders exhibit in a certain way that is mostly unamenable to change across situations. With regard to leadership theory, the two main types of leadership style that are relevant to this dissertation research are the task-oriented and relationship-oriented styles. Each style has benefits, and it is important to learn whether Afghan American males and females are more task-oriented or relationship-oriented given that the impact of a leader on corresponding followers exists along both task and relationship orientations (Northouse, 2004).

The second theme that emerged from the literature was transnationalism. The term transnationalism was first cited in 1916 by American writer Randolph Bourne in the paper entitled *Trans-National America*. The theme is important to the topic of this study because Afghan Americans are originally from Afghanistan but have started new lives in the United States. Vertovec (1999) explained that transnationalism broadly refers to multiple ties and interactions, which link people or institutions across the borders of nation-states.

As a result of transnationalism, Afghans experienced acculturation that refers to the changes arising from intercultural contact (Oudenhoven & Ward, 2013). National culture has long been recognized as a key environmental characteristic underlying systematic differences in administrative behavior (Steenkamp, 2001). Cultural norms and beliefs are influential forces affecting individual perceptions, dispositions and behaviors (Markus & Kitayama, 1991). As researchers started to apply a cross-cultural lens to administrative research, the particulars of culture started to emerge (Lo et al., 2017). For example, Triandis et al. (1988) stated, "Culture is a fuzzy construct" indicating that understanding culture in any socio-psychological context requires an understanding of dimensions of cultural variation (p. 323). The origin of cross-cultural administrative research was established from this point of understanding of cultural dimensions.

In regard to culture, Hofstede (1984) developed theory (i.e., Hofstede's Cultural Dimension Theory) for better understanding a number of cultural dimensions. According to Kirkman et al. (2006), the cultural classification of Geert Hofstede represented the most influential national culture framework in business literature and inspired thousands of empirical studies. Hofstede's model of cultural dimensions has become the most widely accepted and most frequently cited model for cross-cultural research (Al Anezi & Al Ansanri, 2016). Hofstede analyzed data from 88,000 IBM employees from 72 countries and 20 languages, conducted vital studies concerning cultural value dimensions, and established nation-state differences between these dimensions (Hofstede, 2001). As such, Hofstede classified different cultures based upon value dimensions (Nguyen, Mujtaba, & Ruijs, 2014). The Hofstede Cultural Dimension Theory underscores the importance of understanding the differences of culture in the workforce, cross-cultural management, and cross-cultural communication.

Conceptual framework. Figure 1 illustrates the theoretical relationships between predictor variables and leadership style. American acculturation, Afghan acculturation, generation, nursing experience, and sex were expected to predict and explain a significant of leadership orientation, either alone or in combination. Predictor variable are shown on the left of the schematic as input, whereas regression weights are used to fill in the middle of the schematic as process. The outcome on the right of the schematic is leadership style.

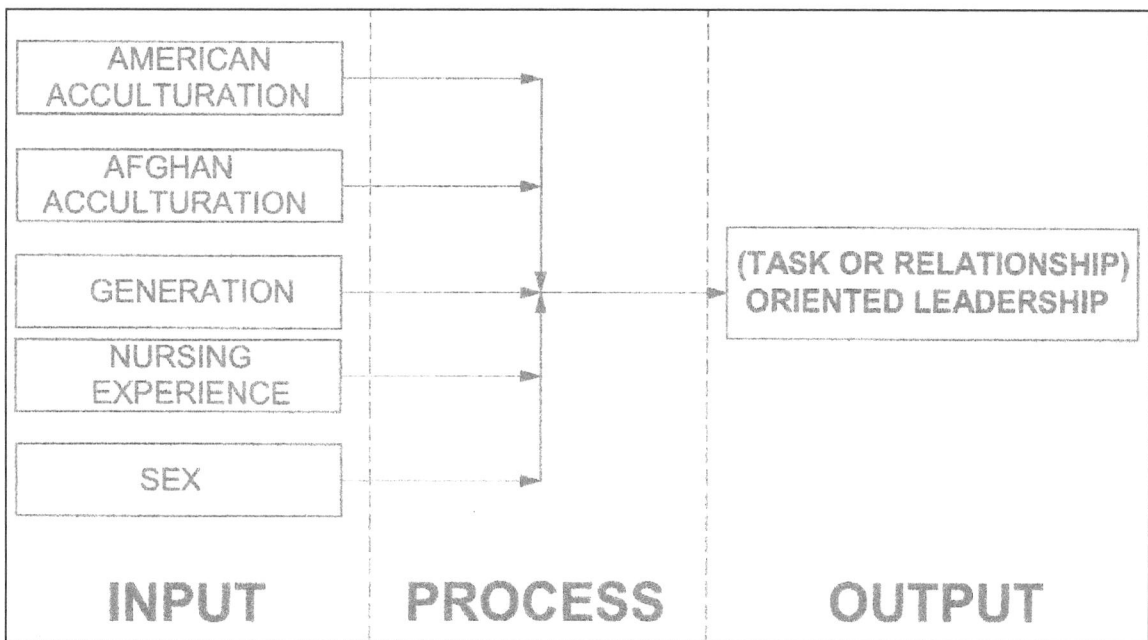

Figure 1. Conceptual framework composed of the predictor variables as input, process measured as regression coefficients, and leadership as output.

43

Hypotheses

H_{01}. There are no significant correlations between acculturation, generation, nursing experience, sex, and task-oriented leadership style.

H_{a1}. There are significant correlations between acculturation, generation, nursing experience, sex, and task-oriented leadership style.

H_{02}. Acculturation, generation, nursing experience, and sex do not collectively predict task-oriented leadership.

H_{a2}. Acculturation, generation, nursing experience, and sex collectively predict task-oriented leadership.

H_{03}. Acculturation, generation, nursing experience, or sex do not make individual unique contributions to predicting task-oriented leadership.

H_{a3}. Acculturation, generation, nursing experience, or sex make individual unique contributions to predicting task-oriented leadership.

H_{04}. There are no significant correlations between acculturation, generation, nursing experience, sex, and relationship-oriented leadership style.

H_{a4}. There are significant correlations between acculturation, generation, nursing experience, sex, and relationship-oriented leadership style.

H_{05}. Acculturation, generation, nursing experience, and sex do not collectively predict relationship-oriented leadership.

H_{a5}. Acculturation, generation, nursing experience, and sex collectively predict relationship-oriented leadership.

H_{06}. Acculturation, generation, nursing experience, or sex do not make individual unique contributions to predicting relationship-oriented leadership.

H_{a6}. Acculturation, generation, nursing experience, or sex make individual unique contributions to predicting relationship-oriented leadership.

Summary

Chapter II focused on the literature that provides a context and evidence foundation for this study. The literature review demonstrated a knowledge gap regarding a lack of knowledge regarding the dominant leadership style of Afghan American nurses in the US healthcare system. The Hofstede Cultural Dimension Theory was used to establish the theoretical orientation of this dissertation thesis and develop the conceptual framework to guide the execution of the dissertation research. The review critically assessed studies on the main variables that were mapped in the conceptual framework and examined in this investigation: (a) leadership style, (b) leadership theory, (c) acculturation, (d) sex, (e) generation, and (f) nursing experience. Although the literature review illustrated a strong connection between culture and leadership, little empirical research exists on how Afghans lead. Certain aspects of the literature on culture and its impact on leader behavior offer promising foundations for future research on Afghan American leadership development. Given the important role culture has on leaders, this study describes how culture, as expressed through acculturation levels, is associated with leadership styles of Afghan American nurses.

Chapter III: Methodology

Afghan American nurses in this quantitative study were surveyed using the Leadership Style Questionnaire (LSQ) to learn if they have an exceptionally high level of task or relationship orientation due to traditional customs and norms. Nurses were also surveyed using the Acculturation Rating Scale (ARS) to see the extent they have acculturated to American customs and norms. The variables of interest to this study were sex, generational affiliation, nursing experience, and acculturation levels. As such, the research methodology of this study used a descriptive correlational quantitative study design.

The purpose of the research was to identify the dominant leadership style among Afghan American nurses working in the US health system and examine its relationships with American and Afghan acculturation, generation, nursing experience, and sex. Acculturation was measured on numeric scales that reflect the extent to which a participant has embraced the American and Afghan cultures, respectively. Generation refers to membership in Generation X or Generation Y groups. Nursing experience was measured in years, and sex was measured as male or female.

Research Design

The goal of this descriptive correlational quantitative study was to explore the predictors of leadership style of Afghan American nurses. The research method was quantitative, and the design was correlational. The goal was to predict task-oriented and relationship-oriented leadership style based upon the variables of sex, generation, work experience, and acculturation.

Population and Sample

      Population. The population was composed of adults with Afghan descent who were at least 18 to 54 years of age, raised in America, and worked in the American healthcare system as registered nurses. Adults of Afghan descent were hereafter labeled Afghan Americans and defined as Afghan nationals who immigrated to the US as children under the age of five years with their Afghan families (native Afghans) or were born into families who immigrated to the US (first generation Afghan Americans).

      Sample. The sample comprised the registered nursing segment of adults of Afghan American descent who currently worked in the United States healthcare system that also met the population characteristics (raised in the United States, at least 18 years of age, and were members of either Gen X or Gen Y born between 1965 and 1994). Data was collected on Registered Nurses (RNs) because CNAs are not necessarily nurses and leadership positions are usually held by RNs and not LVNs or LPNs. Moreover, Nurse Practitioners (NPs) are generally RNs with advanced training (AANP, 2019).

      Power and sample size analysis. Power and sample size analyses were conducted on GPower 3.1.9.2 software to estimate the imputed minimum number of participants to avoid Type II errors. The input parameters were (α = .05), ($1 - \beta$ = .80), and (ES = 0.25). The results showed a minimum sample size range of (n = 180) to (n = 200) participants to achieve sufficient power for this study.

      Sampling procedure. Convenience sampling was used to recruit participants through social media, whereas targeted snowball sampling was recommended for hard-to-reach populations (Dusek, Yurova, & Ruppel, 2015). Assistance was solicited from healthcare colleagues to help recruit participants who were a part of their networks (Appendix B). Participants were invited to participate through postings and advertisements on social media sites and professional networks specific to Afghans (Appendix B). The secondary accessible sample was the Facebook group *Afghan Heath Initiative* composed of over 2,500 Afghan Americans working in healthcare. Using social media improved response rates by reaching the targeted population more "effectively, providing respondents with greater privacy for sensitive questions, providing easier access to the survey, lowering data collection costs and reaching traditionally hard-to-reach populations" (Dusek, Yurova, & Ruppel, 2015, p. 291).

Invitations to participate were sent through postings on the *Afghan Heath Initiative* Facebook group wall that briefly explained the purpose of the study, listed the inclusion criteria, and estimated participation of approximately (5-15 minutes) (Appendix B). The invitation included a link to a SurveyMonkey survey. Interested persons could respond directly on Facebook with questions about participation or the study. Follow-up reminders were posted at one-week intervals. Since the required sample size was not met after two weeks of solicitation, accessible sampling was expanded by inviting people who meet the inclusion criteria on LinkedIn for two additional weeks. Furthermore, assistance was requested from Afghan American community healthcare workers and leaders to help recruit participants who were a part of their communities. As such, the recruitment process took one month. In the event that the necessary sample size was not achieved, the contingency was to consider allowing LVNs and LPNs to participate in the study.

Materials and Instrumentation

The Acculturation and Leadership Survey for Nurses was the primary instrument used to collect data for this study. More specifically, the Acculturation and Leadership Survey for Nurses was a combination of the Leadership Style Questionnaire and the Acculturation Rating Scale. The survey instrument, shown in Appendix C, had 53 items with questions (1-9) on participation-qualification and demographics. Of these questions, generational affiliation (hereafter 'generation') was included with two options of either *Generation X* or *Generation Y*. The demographic birth cohort born between 1965 and 1980 was considered *Generation X* or *Gen X*, whereas the demographic cohort born between 1981 and 1994 were considered *Generation Y, Gen Y, or* Millennials. Generation data was collected as the year of birth and experience was collected as the years working as a registered nurse in the US health system. Participant sex was collected by two options of male or female.

Items 10 through 29 on the Acculturation and Leadership Survey for Nurses were taken from the Leadership Style Questionnaire (LSQ) (Northouse, 2004). Data collected with the LSQ have high internal consistency (reliability, $\alpha = 0.90$, Kaiser-Meyer-Olkin coefficient = 0.90). (Bosiok & Novi Sad, 2013). Permission was granted to use the survey (Appendix F). For each leadership item, participants were asked to rate self-perception regarding each statement using a five-point Likert scale ranging from never to always (1 = never, 2 = occasionally, 3 = sometimes, 4 = frequently, 5 = always). Items from 18 to 27 measured task-oriented leadership, whereas items 28 to 37 measured relationship-oriented leadership (Appendix F). Numerical responses were summated for each leadership style and the total of the summated scores were also interpreted categorically (10-24 = very low; 25-29 = low; 30-34 = moderately low; 35-39 = moderately high; 40-44 = high; 45-50 = very high).

Items 30 to 53 on the Acculturation and Leadership Survey for Nurses measured acculturation. After obtaining permission, each item from the Cuéllar et al. (1995) Acculturation Rating Scale Questionnaire for Hispanics and Latinos (ARSMA-II) was adapted and modified for Afghan Americans (Appendix G). Data collected with the ARSMA have good internal consistency (reliability, $\alpha = 0.93$; Pearson coefficient, $r = 0.89$) (Jimenez et al., 2010). For acculturation, participants were asked to rate self-perception regarding each statement using a five-point Likert scale of frequency (1 = not at all; 2 = very little or not very often; 3 = moderately; 4 = more or very often; 5 = extremely often or almost always). Items 38 to 49 measured American acculturation, whereas items 50 to 61 measured Afghan acculturation. The 12 items associated with American and Afghan acculturation, respectively, were summed in total out of 60 possible points with the total scores interpreted as numbers.

Variables and Operational Definitions

Table 4 shows the operational definitions for the variables in (RQ1-5) for task-oriented leadership. Table 5 shows the operational definitions for the variables in (RQ6-10) for relationship-oriented leadership. The variables listed on Tables 4 and 5 were appropriate given that the purpose of this research was to identify the dominant leadership style among working Afghan American registered nurses and to examine relationships between leadership style and American and Afghan acculturation, generation, nursing experience, and sex. Correlations showed the strength and direction of relationships but did not establish direction of causation, if any, so are labeled as dependent variables (Tabachnick & Fidell, 2019).

Task- and relationship-orientation were measured on an interval scale in which 10 survey items were summed for an overall score from 10 to 50 in value. The score data were correlated with five variables (American acculturation, Afghan acculturation, generation, nursing experience, and sex). Acculturation was measured on an interval scale in which 12 survey items were summed for an overall score ranging from 12 to 60 in value. Nursing experience in years was also measured on an interval scale. For the correlations, sex was dummy coded.

50

Table 4

Operational Definition of Variables: Task-oriented Leadership

Variable	Type	LoM	Values
Task-oriented score	Dependent	Interval	10-50
			1 = never
			5 = always
American acculturation	Dependent	Interval	12-60
			1 = not at all
			5 = often
Afghan acculturation	Dependent	Interval	12-60
			1 = not at all
			5 = often
Generational affiliation	Dependent	Interval	Year of birth
Nursing experience	Dependent	Interval	Years
Sex	Dependent	Nominal	0 = Male
			1= Female

Note. Appendix C contains the survey.

Table 5

Operational Definitions of Variables: Relationship-Oriented Leadership

Variable	Type	LoM	Values
Relationship-orientated score	Dependent	Interval	10-50
			1 = never
			5 = always
American acculturation	Dependent	Interval	12-60
			1 = not at all
			5 = often
Afghan acculturation	Dependent	Interval	12-60
			1 = not at all
			5 = often
Generational affiliation	Dependent	Interval	Year of birth

Nursing experience	Dependent	Interval	Number of Years
Sex	Dependent	Nominal	0 = Male
			1= Female

Note. Appendix C contains the survey.

Data Collection and Statistical Analysis

After obtaining university IRB approval, the researcher complied with guidelines established for the ethical treatment and protection of all participants.

Data collection. Appendix B contains the letter of invitation posted on social media (e.g., Facebook and LinkedIn) that participants received prior to data collection. Individuals who expressed an interest in participating clicked the link in the invitational letter to access the online survey hosted by the SurveyMonkey platform. Data collection utilized best practices for the ethical treatment of research participants by ensuring that each participant understood the purpose of this study and their rights as participants before issuing informed consent.

Consent form. The first page of the survey included a brief introduction to the study and request to agree with the letter of informed consent (Appendix H). The consent form set forth the purpose of the study, the volunteer nature of participation, confidentiality procedures that protect participant information, and participant rights to decline answering any questions or withdraw at any time without penalty. The consent further informed participants of the benefits of participation but were otherwise uncompensated and that they may receive a final report upon request. The consent form was written in language that was accessible and understandable by healthcare workers. Participants were asked to agree to the consent form before data collection began and after consent was received the participants were allowed to access and complete the survey.

Statistical analysis. The statistical analysis included three levels of assessment. First, descriptive statistics were estimated for each variable (univariate) with measures such as central tendency and variance that were either illustrated in graphs or listed in tables. Second, bivariate Pearson correlations were estimated on pairs of variables between each leadership orientation and American and Afghan acculturation, sex, generational affiliation, and amount of nursing experience. Third, based upon the findings in the bivariate analysis, two multiple regressions were conducted to identify the variables that predicted task-oriented leadership and relationship-oriented leadership, respectively. Table 6 shows the analyses of (RQ1-2) for task-oriented leadership. Table 7 shows the analyses of (RQ3-4) for relationship-oriented leadership.

Table 6

Analyses of RQ1 and RQ2

DV (LoM)	IV (LoM)	Statistical Test
RQ1. What are correlations between acculturation, generation, nursing experience, participant sex, and task-oriented leadership style.		
American acculturation (interval)	Task-oriented leadership (interval)	Pearson correlation
Afghan acculturation (interval)	Task-oriented leadership (interval)	Pearson correlation
Generation (interval)	Task-oriented leadership (interval)	Pearson correlation
Nursing experience (interval)	Task-oriented leadership (interval)	Pearson correlation
Sex (nominal)	Task-oriented leadership (interval)	Pearson correlation
RQ2. Do acculturation, generation, nursing experience, and sex predict task-oriented leadership?		
Task-oriented leadership (interval)	American acculturation (interval)	Multiple regression
	Afghan acculturation (interval)	
	Generation (interval)	
	Nursing experience (interval)	
	Sex (nominal)	

Table 7

Analyses of RQ3 and RQ4

DV (LoM)	IV (LoM)		Statistical Test
RQ3. What are the correlations between acculturation, generation, nursing experience, sex, and relationship-oriented leadership style?			
American Acculturation (interval)	Relationship-oriented (interval)	leadership	Pearson correlation
Afghan Acculturation (interval)	Relationship-oriented (interval)	leadership	Pearson correlation
Generation (interval)	Relationship-oriented (interval)	leadership	Pearson correlation
Nursing Experience (interval)	Relationship-oriented (interval)	leadership	Pearson correlation
Sex (nominal)	Relationship-oriented (interval)	leadership	Pearson correlation

RQ4. Do acculturation, generation, nursing experience, and sex predict relationship-oriented leadership?		
Relationship-oriented leadership (interval)	American Acculturation (interval)	Multiple regression
	Afghani Acculturation (interval)	
	Generation (interval)	
	Nursing Experience (interval)	

Assumptions

The untested assumptions were that participants are of Afghan descent, worked in direct patient care in healthcare, were candid when responding, and completed the survey themselves without interference from others. A final assumption was that nurses would not view their responses as admissions of any professional inadequacies.

Limitations

Limitations of the current study include Afghan American nurses' willingness to participate in the research due to a lack of understanding of the benefits of academic research, and lack of external verification that each participant actually was a nurse of Afghan descent and responded with candor. Limitations further consist of potential exposure to unique healthcare experiences that affected personal leadership style or willingness to disclose leadership style honestly. For example, given that a participant with a dominant task-oriented leadership style made past decisions that led to a negative patient outcome and, subsequently, that participant changed to a relationship-orientation as a result, information such as this was not solicited.

The present study generated a sample of participants who provided self-reported data. Self-reported data are artificial to some extent in that they do not measure participant behavior directly in the typical environment where it occurs (Gliner & Morgan, 2000). Participant awareness of 'being studied' also frequently influences self-reported data (Gliner & Morgan, 2000). Awareness of this type easily invokes the social desirability bias, that is, it engenders an intrinsic desire of participants to appear socially acceptable to the researcher despite assurances of anonymity (Gliner & Morgan, 2000). The social desirability bias is likely to be relevant to leadership behavior in the healthcare setting because of social pressure among healthcare professionals to present subject matter expertise given that lives are at stake. Given the sensitivity about lawsuits in healthcare, another limitation was that healthcare workers may feel tempted to cover for something, such as the true quality of their manner at work or what they may believe to be their own medical shortcomings. However, to limit social desirability bias, direct observation did not occur when each participant completed the survey and lengths were taken to formulate and present the survey questions as neutral as possible (Krumpal, 2013). A different limitation was that this research only

55

examined task and relationship-oriented leadership styles based upon the Leadership Style Questionnaire. Finally, a potential limitation was that the principal investigator of this study shared the same nationality as the participants that were studied, which influenced the results in an unknown manner.

Delimitations

The first delimitation of this research was the decision to study the effect of acculturation on leadership among persons of Afghan descent. The second delimitation was the choice to study registered nurses working in direct patient care in the US health system. The third delimitation involved narrowing the focus of the analysis by studying the two birth cohorts Gen X and Gen Y. By focusing on Afghan Gen X and Gen Y, Afghan baby boomers were excluded because many of them came to the US as refugees after the Soviet invasion of Afghanistan and were unable to obtain employment in healthcare or other industries due to language and cultural barriers (Aseel, 2003).

Ethical Assurances

IRB approval was obtained and informed consent was taken before the recruitment of participants and any data was collected to comply with guidelines established for the ethical treatment and protection of participants. Participants were invited to participate with a letter of invitation (Appendix B) that was posted on two websites (e.g., Facebook and LinkedIn). Individuals who expressed an interest in participating clicked the link in the invitational letter to access the online survey set up on SurveyMonkey. Best practices for the ethical treatment of research participants were followed by ensuring that all the participants understood the purpose of the study and their rights as participants.

Consent form. The first page of the survey was a brief introduction to the study and a request to agree with the letter of informed consent (Appendix H and Appendix C). The consent form set forth the purpose of the study, the volunteer nature of participation, confidentiality procedures that protect participants' information, and their rights to decline to answer any questions or withdraw at any time without penalty. It further informed participants of the benefits of participation but were otherwise uncompensated and that they may receive a final report upon request. The consent form was written in a language that was accessible and understandable by healthcare workers. Data collection commenced when each participant formally consented and were fully informed to take part in the research.

Participants in survey research tend to answer survey items more accurately when they believe that their responses are anonymous and cannot be traced to them (Gliner & Morgan, 2000). Therefore, this study involved a professional and potentially personal phenomenon: personal leadership style in carrying out professional duties that directly impact the physical welfare of other people and perhaps whether they live or die. The personal nature of this study necessitated confidentiality as a priority. The entirety of information that could identify individual persons (such as computer IP addresses, which is standard information on SurveyMonkey.com survey results) were replaced with a case number. In addition, the entirety of the collected data remained in a secured and password-protected computer and the sole access to the data, computer securing the data, and the password was the principal investigator. Survey data was downloaded from SurveyMonkey.com as an excel file. The entirety of the collected data and files containing analyses remain confidential and made available only to the principal investigator. Data was stored on a password protected hard drive that will remain in a locked file cabinet for five years following the completion of the study. Aligning to ethical research practices, the data was scheduled to be manually erased at five years after study completion.

Summary

        The goal of this study was to explore the predictors of leadership style of Afghan American nurses. A correlational quantitative design and methodology was selected as the optimal approach to investigate the variables of this study. The population of interest was Afghan Americans that were raised in America and worked in the American healthcare industry. The sample comprised Afghan Americans that worked as nurses in direct patient care and were members of the Gen X and Gen Y cohorts, which were sampled through a combination of convenience and snowball sampling through various social media and professional association outlets. The data collection instrument, *The Acculturation and Leadership Survey for Nurses*, contained 61 items that measured standard demographic variables, task-and relationship-oriented leadership, levels of acculturation to American and Afghan cultures, membership to Gen X or Gen Y birth cohorts, years of nursing experience, and sex. Each participant was assumed to meet the criteria for inclusion into the study. Limitations involved the impracticality of verifying that assumptions were met, whereas the delimitations were the selection of Afghan Americans nurses in Gen X or Gen Y birth cohorts that were currently employed in the US healthcare system. Standard procedures were followed to assure ethical treatment of the participants and protect the confidentiality of participant data.

Chapter IV: Data Analysis and Results

The purpose of this study was to evaluate the interaction between leadership styles and cultural values in the US healthcare setting. The leadership styles of interest were task-oriented leadership and relationship-oriented leadership. Cultural values were measured as Afghan acculturation and American acculturation. The study population was Afghan Americans and participants were Afghan American healthcare nurses. Related demographic characteristics were included, such as sex and nursing experience. The aim of the study was to determine if and how leadership-cultural interaction manifested in the US healthcare setting. The study results are organized in sections around the research questions with data screening covered first followed by descriptive statistics for the demographics, leadership, and acculturation variables, results addressing the four research questions, and a brief evaluation of the findings.

Data Screening

A total of 185 individuals originally agreed to complete the survey and met the inclusion criteria by answering yes to the following three elimination questions: (a) Are you at least 18 years old?, (b) Were one or both of your parents originally from Afghanistan?, and (c) Are you a registered nurse currently practicing in the US Healthcare System? Initial screening for missing values showed that 13 individuals either failed to provide their year of birth (information that was used to identify the participant's generation and therefore essential to this study) or to provide responses to any survey items after the consent form, which necessitated removal from the study.

Data were then screened for entry errors and missing data points. No entry errors were observed since the data were collected with an online survey. There were scattered missing data points, but they did not show any systematic pattern. Likert-scaled responses were screened for normality, linearity, homoscedasticity, and outliers (Tabachnick & Fidell, 2019). Using the definition of an outlier beyond 1.5 *IQR*, screening indicated that case 50 was an outlier compared to the rest of the observations because it had extreme scores on three out of the four primary of this study; hence, this observation was removed from the analysis (Tabachnick & Fidell, 2019). Specifically, case 50 was an outlier for the following reasons:

1. It was a very low outlier on the Afghan Acculturation variable, scoring only seven points after leaving several survey items blank with a range of 12 to 60 points;

2. It was a low outlier on the American acculturation variable, scoring 23 points with a range of values from 12 to 60 points;

3. It was a low outlier on the Relationship-oriented Leadership variable, scoring 11 points with a range of 10 to 50 points; and

4. Upon removal of case 50, the data distributions were statistically normal.

The final sample included ($n = 171$) participants, which was very close to the ($n = 180$) minimum sample size estimated in the power and sample size analysis. The remaining data had no substantial or systematic departures from normality and were treated as continuous data to facilitate parametric inferential Pearson correlations and multiple regression. However, violations of normality assumptions do not create major interpretive problems with large samples defined as those over 40 observations, which reinforces the use of parametric tests on sufficient samples even if the data are found to be non-normal (Ghasemi & Zahediasl, 2012). The distribution of the data can be ignored for samples consisting of hundreds of data points, as in the current study, because sampling distributions are normal regardless of the distribution of the source data and the means of samples from any distribution have normal distributions as per the central limit theorem (Ghasemi & Zahediasl, 2012).

Reliability checks were run with Cronbach's alpha (α) on the four scales composed of conceptually related survey items: (a) task-oriented leadership, (b) relationship-oriented leadership, (c) American acculturation, and (d) Afghan acculturation. Values of Cronbach's α range from zero to one. The closer Cronbach's alpha is to one, the greater the reliability of the database. Indices of ($\alpha \geq .70$) reflect an adequately reliable database.

After screening for reliability, a summated scale was each generated for each scale (task-oriented leadership, relationship-oriented leadership, American acculturation, and Afghan acculturation). A summated scale is a single empirical measure that represents multiple aspects of a construct in one variable (Hair et al., 2010). Deriving a single measure from several related aspects decreases the measurement error in the original data points; this increases data reliability and validity (Hair et al., 2010). Summated scales also increase parsimony in the overall number of variables. Summated scales allowed for comparison relationships between leadership and acculturation among Afghan American nurses at the suitable level of accuracy as well as complexity. A summated scale produces a numeric score for each participant that is either the sum or the mean of the numeric values of the survey items associated with the construct (Tabachnick & Fidell, 2019). In the current study, the sum of the numeric values of the responses was used.

Inferential tests used in this study included correlations and regression. Correlations were run as Pearson product-moment correlations. The correlations were categorically interpreted as (a) small effects, $r = .10$, (b) medium effects, $r = .30$, and (c) large effects, $r = .50$, following the suggestions of Cohen (1988, p. 79-81). It is generally recommended that sample sizes be at least ($n = 100$) when correlations are used to have adequate statistical power and to minimize outlier effects (Warner, 2013). Multiple regression was used with acculturation, generation, nursing experience, and participant sex entered as potential independent or predictor variables, and leadership style serving as the dependent or predicted variable. Regression requires extensive screening to ensure that the data meet the statistical assumptions. The statistical significance threshold was set at $\alpha = .05$. Bonferroni adjustments of the alpha level were not applied because they tend to be too constrictive increasing the chances of Type II errors (Warner, 2013). Data were analyzed with SPSS v 25, a dedicated statistical software.

Descriptive Statistics

Descriptive statistics are presented in three sections: (a) professional demographics, (b) leadership scores, and (c) acculturation scores. Members of the two generations were approximately split with slightly more Gen Y participants. Participants were also approximately similarly split by birth country, with somewhat more participants born in Afghanistan than in the United States (Table 8). About a third had less than five years of nursing experience and the remaining participants had over five years of nursing experience. The majority of participants were registered nurses (Table 8). Those whose job titles fell under the 'other' category included Certified Registered Nurse Anesthetist (CRNA), Nurse Practitioner (NP), and Post Doc Fellow in Nursing. The proportions of males and females were approximately split, whereas the majority of participants held undergraduate degrees compared to graduate degrees.

Table 8

Professional Demographic Descriptive Statistics

Variable ($n = 171$)	N	$\%$
Generation (year range)		
Gen X (1965 - 1980)	72	42.1
Gen Y (1981 - 1994)	99	57.9
Birth country		
United States	78	45.6
Afghanistan	93	54.4

Nursing experience		
< 5 years	50	29.2
> 5 years	121	70.8
Job title		
Registered nurse	157	91.8
Other	14	8.2
Sex		
Male	84	49.1
Female	87	50.9
Highest educational level		
2-Year college degree	46	26.8
4-Year college degree	107	62.6
Some graduate school	3	1.8
Graduate degree	15	8.8

Table 8 shows that the participant pool was approximately split between men and women, and between members of Gen X and Gen Y. A chi-square test of independence was run to determine if there were equal numbers of men and women in the two generations. The chi-square test showed that sex and generation were significantly associated, $\chi^2 (1, 171) = 15.32, p < .011, \Phi = .30, p < .001$, with significantly more Gen X men (48 men vs. 24 women, $z = 3.9$) and significantly more Gen Y women (63 women vs. 36 men, $z = 3.9$).

Figure 2 illustrates these differences:

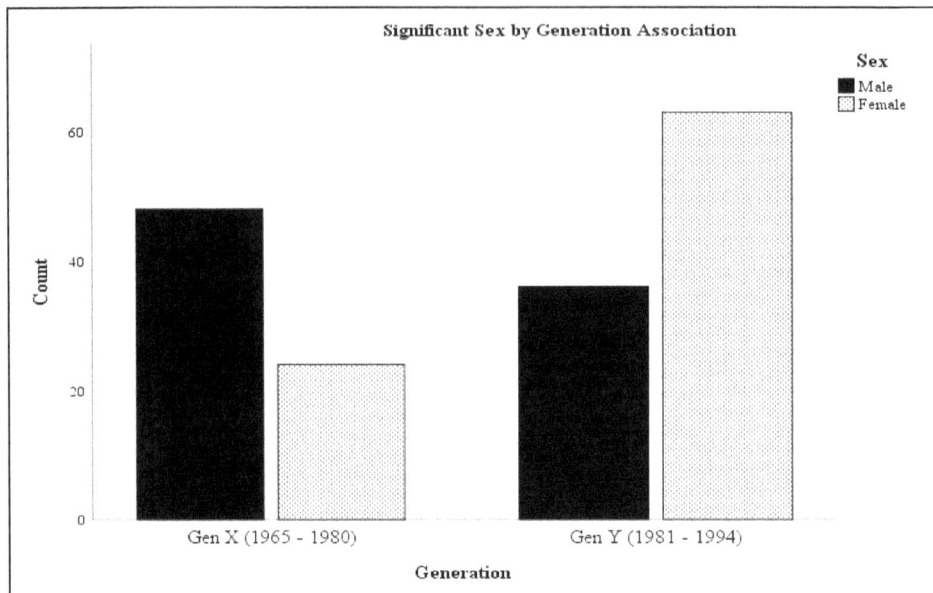

Figure 2. Significant association of sex by generation.

Leadership descriptive statistics. Table 10 shows the descriptive statistics for the participant leadership scores. As mentioned above, the minimum and maximum possible scores were from 10 to 50 (10 survey items measured with a 5-point frequency scale, 1 = never, 5 = always). Cronbach's α statistics listed on Table 10 showed that both task-oriented and relationship-oriented leadership data were highly reliable.

The mean score of task-oriented leadership was 35, which indicated that, on average, participants used task-oriented leadership behaviors 'sometimes.' The minimum score was 15, and this was close to the possible minimum of 10 that corresponded to 'never' using task-oriented leadership. The maximum statistic that some participants reported was that they 'always' use task-oriented leadership behaviors.

64

The mean score of relationship-oriented leadership was 39, which was four points higher than the task-oriented leadership mean score (Table 9). The value was approximately 10 points away from the maximum leadership value of 50.

Table 9

Participant Leadership Descriptive Statistics

Statistic ($n = 171$)		Leadership Scores	
		Task	Relationship
Cronbach's α		.904	.952
M (SE)		35.40 (0.56)	39.27 (0.62)
95% CI	UL	34.28	38.04
	LL	36.52	40.50
5% Trimmed M		35.66	39.68
Median		36.00	42.00
Variance		54.80	66.01
SD		7.40	8.12
Minimum		15.00	17.00
Maximum		50.00	50.00
Range		35.00	33.00
IQR		10.00	10.00
Skewness		-.37	-.78
Kurtosis		-.49	-.37

Acculturation descriptive statistics. Table 10 lists the participant descriptive statistics for acculturation. The possible range of acculturation scores for both American and Afghanistan acculturation was 12 to 60, which located the median of that range at 36 and corresponded to a rate of exhibiting a particular culture's behaviors 'moderately often.' Cronbach's α statistics on both the Afghan acculturation and American acculturation variables showed that the acculturation data were highly reliable. The Afghanistan acculturation mean of 38.93 in Table 10 indicated that participants said that they exhibited

Afghan cultural behaviors 'moderately often' on average. The American acculturation mean of 47.03 in Table 10 indicated that participants said that they exhibited American cultural behaviors 'very often' on average. The trimmed means for frequency of the two cultural expressions were similar in value, indicating a general absence of extreme values at the high and low ends of the data. Similar values of the respective standard deviations showed that the American and Afghan data were comparably variable.

Table 10

Participant Acculturation Descriptive Statistics

		Acculturation	
Statistic (*n* = 171)		Afghan	American
Cronbach's α		.944	.838
M (*SE*)		38.98 (0.62)	47.03 (0.56)
95% *CI*	*LL*	37.75	45.92
	UL	40.21	48.14
5% trimmed *M*		39.00	47.26
Median		39.00	48.00
Variance		66.52	53.86
SD		8.15	7.33
Minimum		19.00	25.00
Maximum		60.00	60.00
Range		41.00	35.00
IQR		11.00	12.00
Skewness		-.01	-.48
Kurtosis		-.30	-.20

Table 11 lists the mean scores for task- and relationship-oriented leadership and for Afghan and American acculturation by demographic characteristic. The most striking differences between means emerged for relationship-oriented leadership and American acculturation. Specifically, distinguishing demographic characteristics for relationship-oriented leadership and American acculturation included generation, birth country, job title, and education. Distinguishing demographic characteristics for relationship-oriented leadership included sex and years in health care.

Table 11

Leadership and Acculturation by Demographic Characteristics

Demographic characteristic	Leadership		Acculturation	
	Task	Relationship	Afghan	American
Generation	M (SD)	M (SD)	M (SD)	M (SD)
Gen X (1965-1980)	36.19 (8.01)	36.43 (8.74)	39.79 (8.39)	44.51 (7.95)
Gen Y (1981-1994)	34.82 (6.90)	41.34 (6.99)	38.40 (7.97)	48.86 (6.29)
Birth country				
United States	35.37 (7.00)	41.61 (7.28)	38.64 (8.48)	50.01 (5.60)
Afghanistan	35.43 (7.75)	37.31 (8.31)	39.27 (7.90)	44.53 (7.71)
Nursing experience				
< 5 Years	33.94 (7.41)	42.42 (6.26)	40.00 (8.16)	48.52 (6.99)
> 5 Years	36.00 (7.34)	37.97 (8.46)	38.57 (8.14)	46.42 (7.42)
Job title				
Registered nurse	35.42 (7.41)	38.79 (8.25)	38.80 (7.89)	46.68 (7.43)
Other	35.14 (7.56)	44.64 (3.53)	41.00 (10.82)	51.00 (4.73)
Sex				
Male	38.17 (6.96)	35.38 (9.24)	38.09 (8.48)	46.03 (7.85)
Female	32.72 (6.83)	43.03 (4.35)	39.85 (7.77)	48.00 (6.71)
Highest educational level				
2-Year college degree	36.00 (8.36)	35.78 (9.08)	38.30 (8.64)	45.71 (7.14)
4-Year college degree	34.82 (7.24)	40.14 (7.69)	39.57 (8.02)	47.05 (7.69)
Some graduate school	36.00 (7.00)	41.00 (3.00)	39.33 (7.76)	46.33 (2.31)
Graduate degree	37.60 (5.21)	43.40 (4.70)	36.80 (7.89)	51.06 (4.14)

Bivariate and Multivariate Analysis

    RQ 1. What are the correlations between acculturation, generation, nursing experience, sex, and task-oriented leadership style?

    H₀. There are no significant correlations between acculturation, generation, nursing experience, sex, and task-oriented leadership style.

    H₁. There are significant correlations between acculturation, generation, nursing experience, sex, and task-oriented leadership style.

    Bivariate analyses for task-oriented leadership. Table 12 lists the correlations between the variables: American acculturation, Afghan acculturation, generation, nursing experience, participant sex, and task-oriented leadership style above the blank diagonal line. Statistically significant correlations are shown in bold; the null hypothesis was rejected for these.

    The far right-hand vertical column on Table 12 lists the correlations between task-oriented leadership and acculturation, generation, nursing experience, and participant sex. Three statistically significant correlations emerged. The strongest statistically significant correlation involving task-oriented leadership was the negative or inverse correlation with participant sex ($r = -.37$). Given that the dichotomous sex variable was coded in the direction of (0 = male and 1 = female), the inverse correlation showed that men reported more frequent task-oriented leadership than did women. The second strongest statistically significant correlation with task-oriented leadership ($r = .21$) emerged with years of nursing experience (Table 12). The direct correlation indicated that the longer participants had been nursing, the more task-oriented they were. The third strongest significant correlation involving task-oriented leadership emerged with American acculturation (Table 12). The two variables were indirectly but weakly correlated ($r = -.18$), which showed that participants who reported higher task-oriented leadership also reported lower American acculturation scores. The two remaining correlations showed that task-oriented leadership was unrelated to the levels of Afghan acculturation and to generation. The null hypothesis was not rejected for these two correlations. The strengths of the correlations were sufficient to justify running the regression for research question two.

Table 12

Pearson Correlation Matrix: Task-Oriented Relationship

($n = 171$)	V1	V2	V3	V4	V5	V6
V1 Afghan Acculturation		-.44**	-.08	-.05	.11	.13
V2 American Acculturation	0.19		.29**	-.22**	.13	-.18*
V3 Generation	0.01	0.08		-.63**	.30**	-.09
V4 Years Nursing Experience	0.00	0.05	0.40		-.21**	.21**
V5 Sex	0.01	0.02	0.09	0.04		-.37**
V6 Task-oriented Leadership	0.02	0.03	0.01	0.04	.14	

Note. V = variable. Correlation coefficients shown above the blank diagonal line. Coefficients of determination shown below the blank diagonal line. *Correlation is significant at the 0.05 level (2-tailed). **Correlation is significant at the 0.01 level (2-tailed).

Table 12 also shows that a number of significant correlations arose among the potential predictor variables. American and Afghan acculturation were moderately and inversely correlated with each other ($r = -.44$). American acculturation was directly related to generation ($r = .29$). Generation and years of nursing experience were strongly and inversely related ($r = -.63$). Years of nursing experience were correlated with sex ($r = -.21$). The correlations were not strong enough to introduce the problem of excess relationships among the potential predictor variables (called multicollinearity) into the regression for research question two.

Coefficients of determination are shown below the blank diagonal in Table 12 as effect size statistics. There were strong reciprocal effects between generation on nursing experience, on acculturation, and between sex and task-oriented leadership.

Answer to RQ1. Task-oriented leadership correlated significantly with American acculturation, years of nursing experience, and participant sex. Correlations about the potential predictor variables ranged from (-.084) to (-.633).

RQ 2. Do acculturation, generation, nursing experience, and sex predict task-oriented leadership?

Multivariate analyses for task-oriented leadership. Research question two was answered with multiple regression testing of two sets of hypotheses. The first set tested the hypothesis that the regression model, with its addition of predictor variables, was no better at predicting task-oriented leadership than was the mean of task-oriented leadership (Table 9). The specific hypotheses were:

H0. Acculturation, generation, nursing experience, and sex do not collectively predict task-oriented leadership or $R^2 = 0$.

H1. Acculturation, generation, nursing experience, and sex collectively predict task-oriented leadership or $R^2 > 0$.

The second set of hypotheses that regression tested was that the slope of the regression line for each predictor variable was something other than zero (i.e., was not horizontal). The specific hypotheses were:

H0. Acculturation, generation, nursing experience, or sex do not make individual unique contributions to predicting task-oriented leadership or $\beta = 0$.

H1. Acculturation, generation, nursing experience, or sex make individual unique contributions to predicting task-oriented leadership or $\beta \neq 0$.

70

Multiple regression assumptions testing. The first assumption was that the sample size must be adequate. Sample size impacts the statistical power and generalizability of multiple regression analyses. Small samples compromise the power to detect statistically significant relationships and only detect very strong relationships with any degree of certainty. Generalizability is also directly affected by the ratio of participants to independent variables. Tabachnick and Fidell (2019) recommend a minimum of 15 to 20 participants for each independent variable. The database in the current study had ($n = 171$) participants and five potential predictor variables, so sample size was more than adequate to detect relationships and generalize findings.

The second assumption necessitated that the relationships between predicted and predictor variables must be linear. Multiple linear regression is based on a linear relationship between the predictor variables (predictor variables in the current study were American acculturation, Afghan acculturation, generation, nursing experience, and sex) and the dependent variables (in the current study, task-oriented leadership for RQ2 and relationship-oriented leadership for RQ4). The linearity assumption was checked with visual inspection of individual scatter plots of leadership and potential predictors outfitted with superimposed lines of best fit (scatter plots not shown). Each relationship was linear, indicating that the data met this assumption.

The third assumption required that individual variables must show univariate normality; hence, the data were screened for univariate normality. Tables 9 and 10 show that the skewness and kurtosis statistics for the variables were within the ($\pm$ 2) criterion for normality (Warner, 2013). Significance tests of the normality assumption can also be run by generating z scores (by dividing skew and kurtosis statistics by their standard error) and determining if any values fell outside the criterion, $z = 3.29$, $p < .001$ (Tabachnick & Fidell, 2019). Skew and kurtosis significance tests for all the four subscales fell well below, $z =$

3.29. The non-significant results indicated that the data met the regression assumption of univariate normality.

The fourth assumption was that the data must not include outliers because multiple linear regression is very sensitive to outlier effects. The data were screened for outliers and homoscedasticity, while establishing that the error between observed and predicted values (i.e., the residuals of the regression) were normally distributed (Warner, 2013). The assumptions were checked with visual inspection of the Normal P-P plot in Figure 3, the histogram of standardized residuals in Figure 4, and the plot of the standardized residuals by predicted values in Figure 5. After the removal of case 50, visual inspection of Normal P-P plots revealed a normal distribution, absence of outliers, and homoscedasticity (Figure 3). The residual plots showed that the leadership residuals were also normally distributed (Figures 4 and 5).

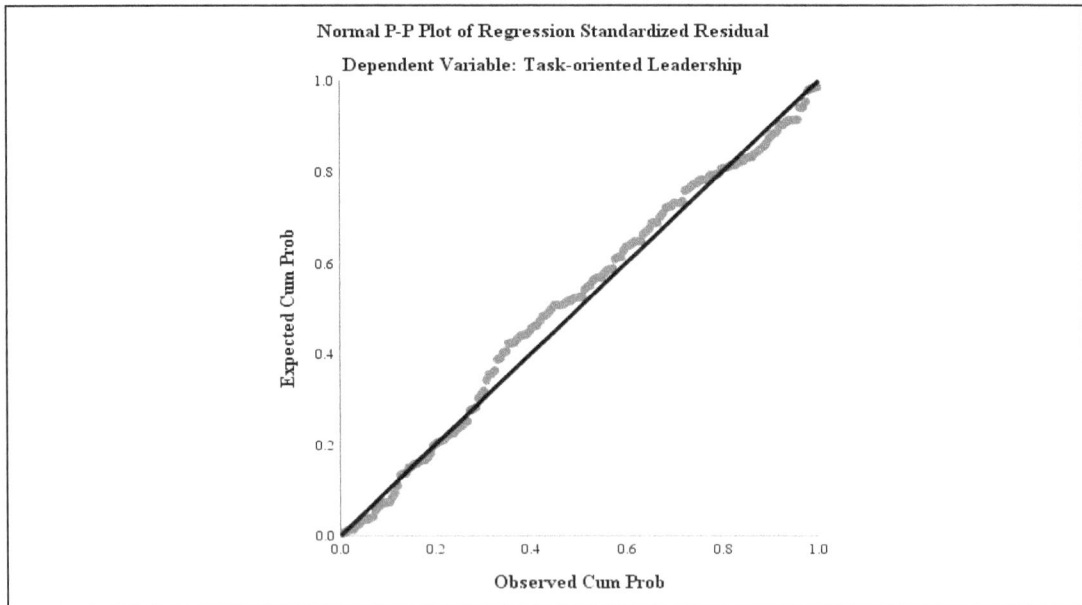

Figure 3. Normal P-P plot of the standardized residual predicting task-oriented leadership plotted against the normal curve.

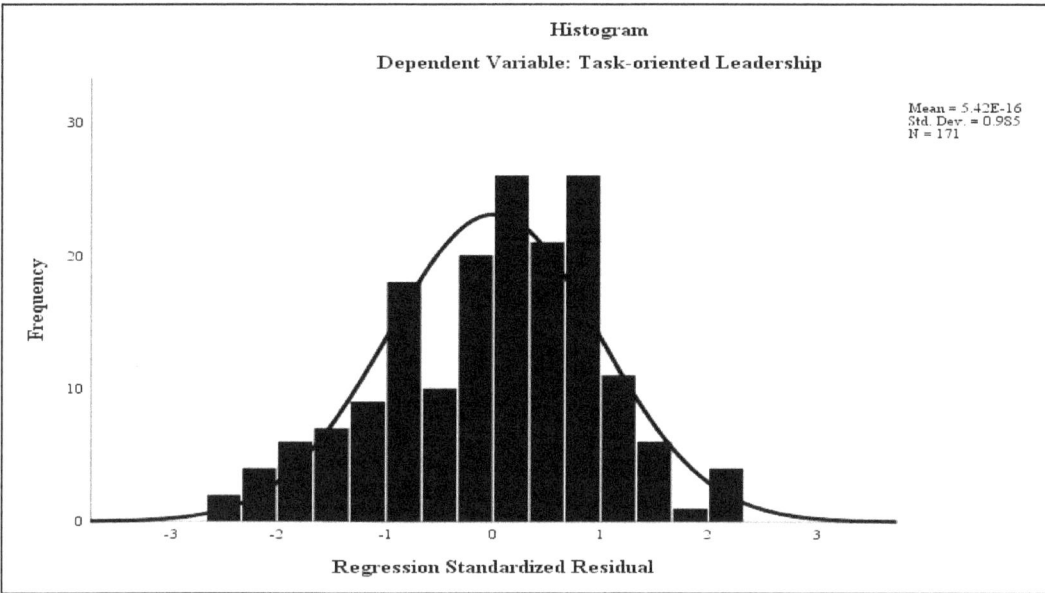

Figure 4. Normally distributed histogram of task-oriented leadership standardized residuals.

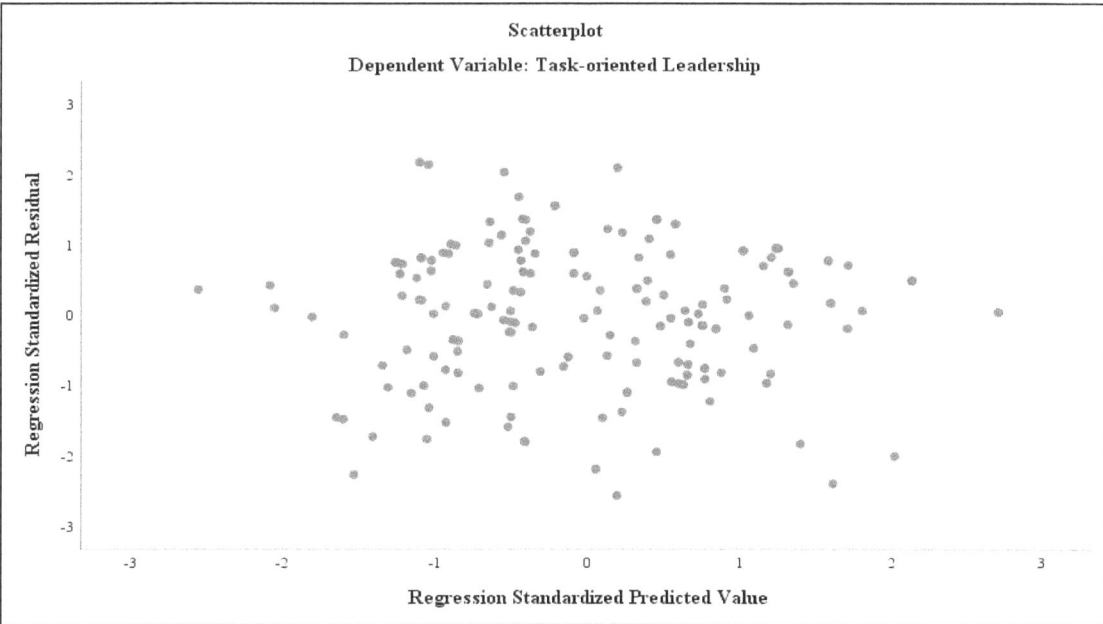

Figure 5. Scatter plot of the standardized residual against the standardized predicted value for task-oriented leadership.

The fifth assumption required that the data must show multivariate normality. Data were screened for multivariate normality with Mahalanobis distances to identify data points that lie substantially outside the swarm of data points in multivariate space using the chi-square distribution (Tabachnick & Fidell, 2019). Mahalanobis distances were generated for all data points. A data point identified any particular case (i.e., participant) as a multivariate outlier if the corresponding χ^2 statistic was a value of 16.75 or greater; the criterion value was based on the critical chi-square value for five predictor variables at $p = .005$ (Tabachnick & Fidell, 2019). No cases (i.e., participants) emerged as multivariate outliers.

The sixth assumption was that predictor variables must not show collinearity or multicollinearity; the independent or predictor variables are not correlated with one another. The collinearity requirement meant that two correlated predictor variables did not show collinearity and more than two predictor variables did not show multicollinearity. The data met this regression assumption based on several criteria. First, the intercorrelations among the potential predictors in Table 12 ranged from .09 to .66. Based on Hair et al. (2010) criterion value that no correlation between American acculturation, Afghan acculturation, generation, nursing experience, and sex was $r = .70$ or more, this suggested that multicollinearity was not an issue when entering all the predictor variables into the regression. Second, the tolerance statistics in Table 13 are large. Tolerance statistics reflect the proportion of variance in the listed predictor variable that is not predictable from or shared with the other predictor variables already in the regression (Tabachnick & Fidell, 2019). Large tolerance values indicated that any relationship between a listed predictor variable (i.e., generation or sex) and transformational leadership was largely unaffected by its relationships with the other predictor variables. The minimum possible tolerance value is zero and a zero value indicates that the predictor variable does not contain any additional variance that is not already present in or shared with the other predictor variables; zero

74

tolerance represents perfect multicollinearity. A variable with zero tolerance cannot add any new predictive information to the regression. If tolerance is less than 0.20 (20%), multicollinearity is possible in the data and when tolerance is less than 0.01 (10%), multicollinearity is an issue. On the other end of the range of values, the maximum possible value of tolerance is one. A tolerance value of one indicates that the predictor variable is completely uncorrelated with the other predictor variables included in the regression. Tolerances that are substantially larger than zero are evidence that the predictor variable contains new information that is not already provided by the other predictor variables. The large tolerance values in Table 13 show that each predictor had the potential to explain a unique proportion of task-oriented leadership, unaffected by relationships it had with the other predictor variables. Lastly, when VIFs are greater than 10, multicollinearity is present (Warner, 2013). The variance inflation factors (VIF; calculated with the formula 1 divided by tolerance) shown on Table 13 were all less than 10.

The seventh assumption required that the data must not be auto correlated. The data met the multiple linear regression assumption of little or no auto correlation, Durbin-Watson $d = 1.67$. The Durbin-Watson test determines whether the residuals are independent of one another. The DW statistic d can assume values in the range of (0-4); however, the rule of thumb is that values in the range of ($1.5 < d < 2.5$) indicate the absence of auto correlation. The task-oriented leadership data met this assumption.

Regression results. The first set of hypotheses was that the regression model (i.e., the addition of American acculturation, Afghan acculturation, generation, nursing experience, or sex) was no better at predicting task-oriented leadership than was the task-oriented leadership mean (H_0: $R^2 = 0$). The hypothesis was rejected, $R^2 = .22$, $F(5, 165) = 9.20$, $p < .001$. The addition of predictors explained a statistically significant 22% variance of task-oriented leadership. Viewing R^2 as an effect size statistic, the combined effect of

American acculturation, Afghan acculturation, generation, nursing experience, or sex exerted sufficient effect to explain 22% of the variance for task-oriented leadership.

The second set of hypotheses was that the slope of the regression line was a value other than zero (i.e., not horizontal, H_0: $\beta = 0$). The null hypothesis predicted that one or more of the predictor variables each made a unique and statistically significant contribution to predicting task-oriented leadership. The t statistics and associated p values in Table 13 showed that four out of the five potential predictor variables independently made a statistically significant and unique contribution to explaining task-oriented leadership among Afghan American nurses. The significant predictors were Afghan acculturation, generation, nursing experience, and participant sex. The hypothesis (H_0: $\beta = 0$) was rejected for these predictors. The analysis failed to reject the null hypothesis for American acculturation. The beta (β) coefficients or weights of the predictor variables are shown in Table 13 showed that the variables are listed in descending order of predictive influence, with participant sex having the most weight in predicting task-oriented leadership, followed by years of nursing experience, generation, and Afghan acculturation.

Table 13

Multiple Regression Coefficients: Task-Oriented Leadership

Model ($n = 171$)	β	SE	β_{Std}	t	p	r	pr	T	VIF
Constant	29.38	6.04		4.86	.000				
Sex	-5.82	1.08	-.39	-5.37	.000	-.36	-.38	.88	1.14
Years Nursing Experience	0.38	0.12	.27	3.07	.002	.21	.23	.58	1.72
Generation	3.50	1.39	.23	2.51	.013	-.09	.19	.54	1.83
Afghan Acculturation	0.16	0.07	.18	2.29	.023	.13	.17	.75	1.33
American Acculturation	-0.05	0.08	-0.05	-0.67	.504	-.18	-.05	.71	1.40

Note. Significant predictors in bold. β and SE statistics are unstandardized coefficients. β_{Std} are standardized coefficients. The statistics, r and pr are zero-order and partial correlations, respectively. T = tolerance and VIF = variance inflation factor are collinearity statistics.

Figures 6 through 9 illustrate the relationships between the significant predictor variables and task-oriented leadership as scatter plots with superimposed lines of best fit.

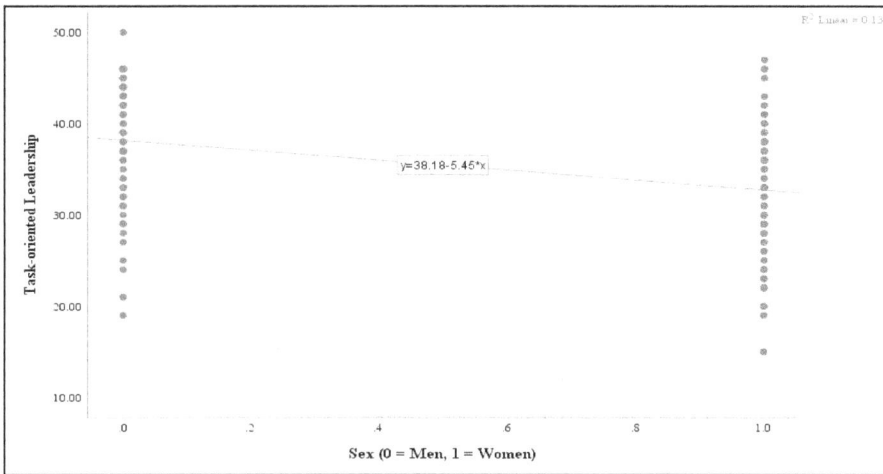

Figure 6. Scatter plot of task-oriented leadership and the predictor variable of participant sex.

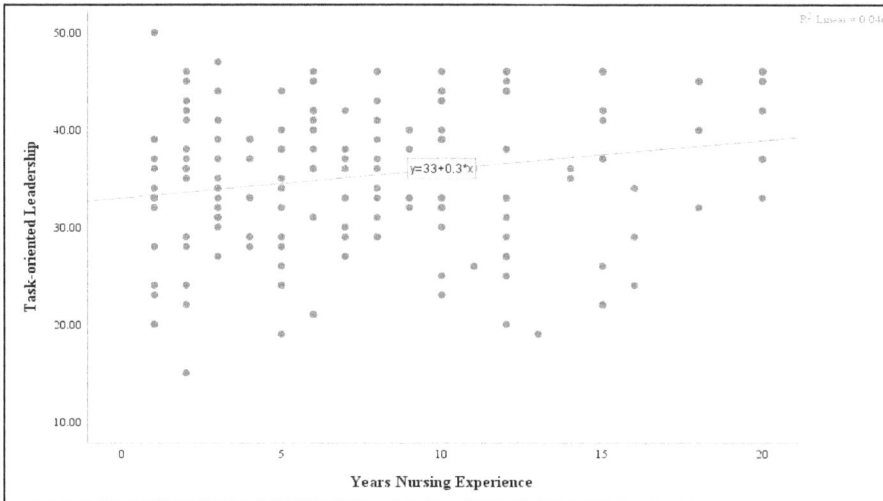

Figure 7. Scatter plot of task-oriented leadership and the predictor variable of years of nursing experience.

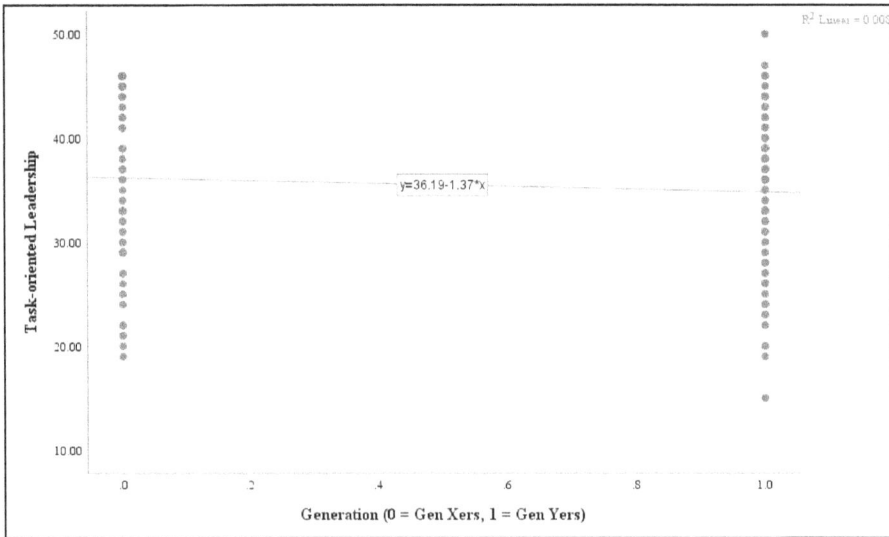

Figure 8. Scatter plot of task-oriented leadership and the predictor variable of generation.

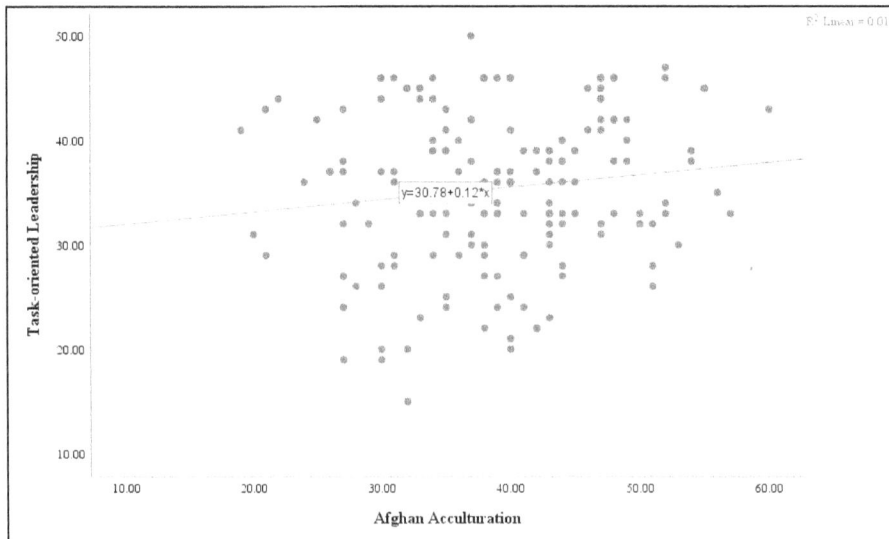

Figure 9. Scatter plot of task-oriented leadership and the predictor variable of Afghan acculturation.

The task-oriented leadership regression model was re-specified without American acculturation. The procedure yielded four separate regression lines that predicted task-oriented leadership, one for each group of men and women in the Gen X and Gen Y birth cohorts, respectively:

1. Gen X men predicted task-oriented leadership score = 25.94 + 0.39(nursing experience) + 0.18(Afghan acculturation).

2. Gen X women predicted task-oriented leadership score = 25.94 − 5.92(sex) + 0.39(nursing experience) + 0.18(Afghan acculturation).

3. Gen Y men predicted task-oriented leadership score = 25.94 + 0.39(nursing experience) + 3.39(generation) + 0.18(Afghan acculturation).

4. Gen Y women predicted task-oriented leadership score = 25.94 − 5.92(sex) + 0.39(years of nursing experience) + 3.39(generation) + 0.18(Afghan acculturation).

Figure 10 illustrates task-oriented leadership means across the four types of participants. The means on the left side of the graph show that men of both generations were more task-oriented (Gen X men, $M = 38.93$, $SD = 7.10$, $n = 48$; Gen Y men, $M = 37.17$, $SD = 6.74$, $n = 36$) than were women (Gen X women, $M = 30.71$, $SD = 6.93$, $n = 24$; Gen Y women, $M = 33.49$, $SD = 6.68$, $n = 63$).

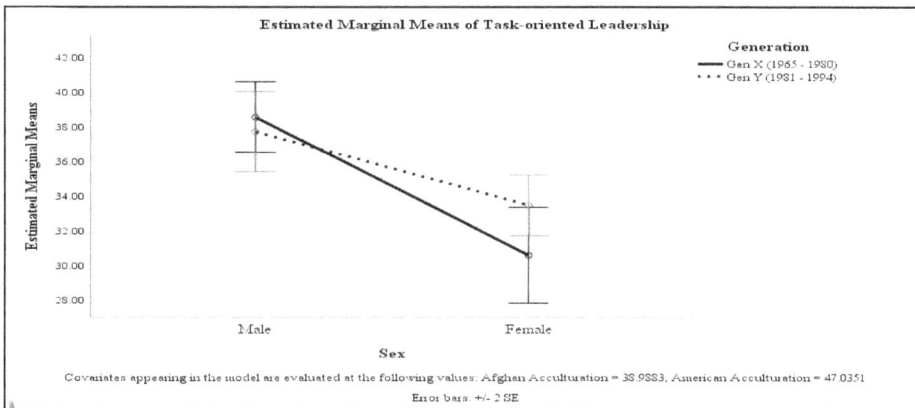

Figure 10. Means of task-oriented leadership by generation and sex.

A post hoc power analysis was run on task-oriented leadership to measure the power of the analysis to avoid a Type II error with GPower software. For the two-tailed test, holding the effect size $R^2 = .22$, $\alpha = .05$, $n = 171$, and four predictors constant, the observed power was $(1 - \beta = .99)$.

Answer to RQ2. Task-oriented leadership was most strongly predicted by the male sex. Men were significantly more task-oriented than were women. In addition, because Gen X men were more closely associated with longer nursing experience and higher levels of Afghan acculturation, these predictor variables also made significant contributions to predicting task-oriented leadership.

RQ3. What are the correlations between acculturation, generation, nursing experience, sex, and relationship-oriented leadership style?

H$_0$. There are no significant correlations between acculturation, generation, nursing experience, sex, and relationship-oriented leadership style.

H$_1$. There are significant correlations between acculturation, generation, nursing experience, sex, and relationship-oriented leadership style.

Bivariate analyses. The Pearson correlation matrix in Table 14 shows the correlations between relationship-oriented leadership and potential predictor variables in the far right-hand vertical column. Each of the predictor variable, relationship-oriented, leadership correlations were statistically significant. The correlation null hypothesis was rejected for each of the five correlations. Four of the correlations were direct. The correlation between relationship-oriented leadership and years of nursing experience was negative. The strength of these correlations, and those between the potential predictor variables (presented in results for RQ1), provided evidence and justification for running the regression for RQ4.

80

Coefficients of determination are shown below the blank diagonal on Table 14 as effect size statistics. There were strong reciprocal effects between generation on nursing experience, acculturation, and between sex and relationship-oriented leadership.

Table 14

Pearson Correlation Matrix: Relationship-Oriented Leadership

($n = 171$)	V1	V2	V3	V4	V5	V6
V1 Afghan Acculturation		$-.44^{**}$	$-.08$	$-.05$	$.11$	$.32^{**}$
V2 American Acculturation	0.19		$.29^{**}$	$-.22^{**}$	$.13$	$.21^{*}$
V3 Generation	0.01	0.08		$-.63^{**}$	$.30^{**}$	$.30^{**}$
V4 Years Nursing Experience	0.00	0.05	0.40		$-.21^{**}$	$-.33^{**}$
V5 Sex	0.01	0.02	0.09	0.04		$.47^{**}$
V6 Relationship-oriented Leadership	0.10	0.04	0.09	0.11	.22	

Note. V = variable. Correlation coefficients shown above the blank diagonal line. Coefficients of determination shown below the blank diagonal line. *Correlation is significant at the 0.05 level (2-tailed). **Correlation is significant at the 0.01 level (2-tailed).

Answer to RQ3. Relationship-oriented leadership correlated significantly with all five potential predictor variables (American acculturation, Afghan acculturation, generation, nursing experience, and participant sex).

RQ4. Do acculturation, generation, nursing experience, and sex predict relationship-oriented leadership?

Multivariate analyses for relationship-oriented leadership. Research question four was addressed with multiple regression. The independent variables were acculturation, nursing experience, generation, and sex. The dependent variable was relationship-oriented leadership. Data assumptions were met for multiple regression and evidence of qualification was presented in section RQ2. Multiple regression was used to test two sets of hypotheses.

H_0. Acculturation, generation, nursing experience, and participant sex do not collectively predict relationship-oriented leadership or $R^2 = 0$.

H_1. Acculturation, generation, nursing experience, and participant sex collectively predict relationship-oriented leadership or $R^2 > 0$.

H_0. Acculturation, generation, nursing experience, or participant sex do not make individual unique contributions to predicting relationship-oriented leadership or $\beta = 0$.

H_1. Acculturation, generation, nursing experience, or participant sex make individual unique contributions to predicting relationship-oriented leadership or $\beta \neq 0$.

Regression results. The first set of hypotheses, H_0: $R^2 = 0$, tested the prediction that the regression model (i.e., collective addition of American acculturation, Afghan acculturation, generation, nursing experience, or sex) was no better at predicting relationship-oriented leadership than was relationship-oriented leadership. The null hypothesis was rejected ($R^2 = .42$, $F(5, 165) = 23.49$, $p < .001$). The addition of predictors explained a statistically significant 42% of relationship-oriented leadership. That is, viewing R^2 as an effect size statistic, the combined effect of American acculturation, Afghan acculturation, generation, nursing experience, and sex exerted sufficient effect to explain 42% of relationship-oriented leadership.

The second regression null hypothesis predicted that one or more of the predictor variables each made a unique and statistically significant contribution to predicting relationship-oriented leadership. The specific prediction was that the slope of the regression line was some value other than zero for the predictors (H_0: $\beta = 0$). The results of the regression are listed in Table 15 and the variables are presented in descending order of predictive weight (β statistics). The t statistics and associated p values showed that Afghan acculturation, participant sex, and American acculturation each made a statistically significant and unique contribution to explaining relationship-oriented leadership among American nurses of Afghan descent. The hypothesis, H_0: $\beta = 0$, was rejected for these three

82

predictors. The analysis failed to reject the null hypothesis for years of nursing experience and generation.

Table 15

Multiple Regression Coefficients: Relationship-Oriented Leadership

Model ($n = 171$)	β	SE	β_{Std}	t	p	r	Pr	T	VIF
Constant	5.99	5.73		1.04	.297				
Afghan Acculturation	0.41	0.07	.41	6.01	.000	.32	.42	.75	1.33
Sex	5.55	1.03	.34	5.39	.000	.47	.39	.87	1.13
American Acculturation	0.32	0.08	.29	4.20	.000	.21	.31	.71	1.40
Generation	1.03	1.32	.06	0.78	.435	.30	.06	.54	1.83
Years Nursing Experience	-0.19	0.12	-.13	-1.64	.101	-.33	-.13	.57	1.72

Note. Significant predictors shown in bold. β and *SE* statistics are unstandardized coefficients. β_{Std} statistics are standardized coefficients. Both *r* and *pr* are zero-order and partial correlations, respectively. *T* = tolerance and *VIF* = variance inflation factor are collinearity statistics.

Figures 11-13 illustrate the significant relationships between the predictor variables and relationship-oriented leadership as scatter plots with superimposed lines of best fit.

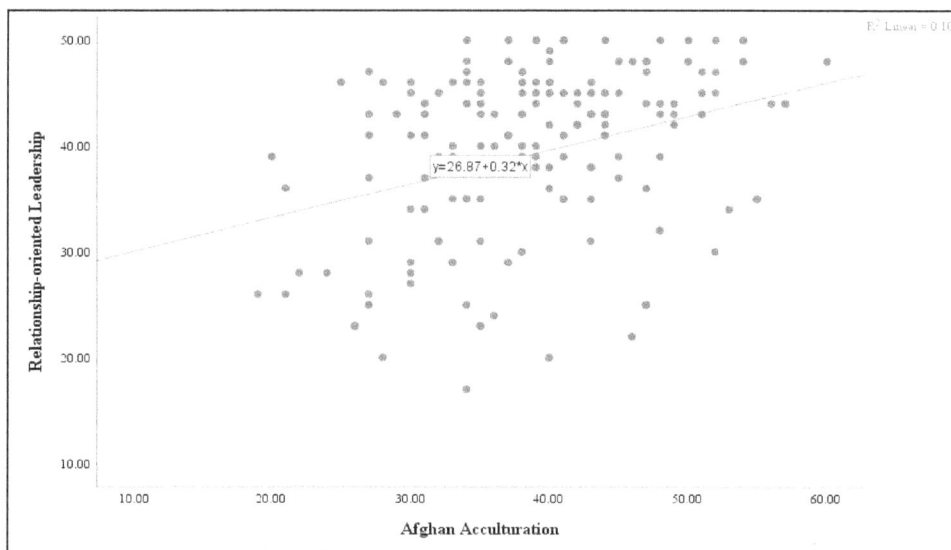

Figure 11. Scatter plot of relationship-oriented leadership and the predictor variable of Afghan acculturation.

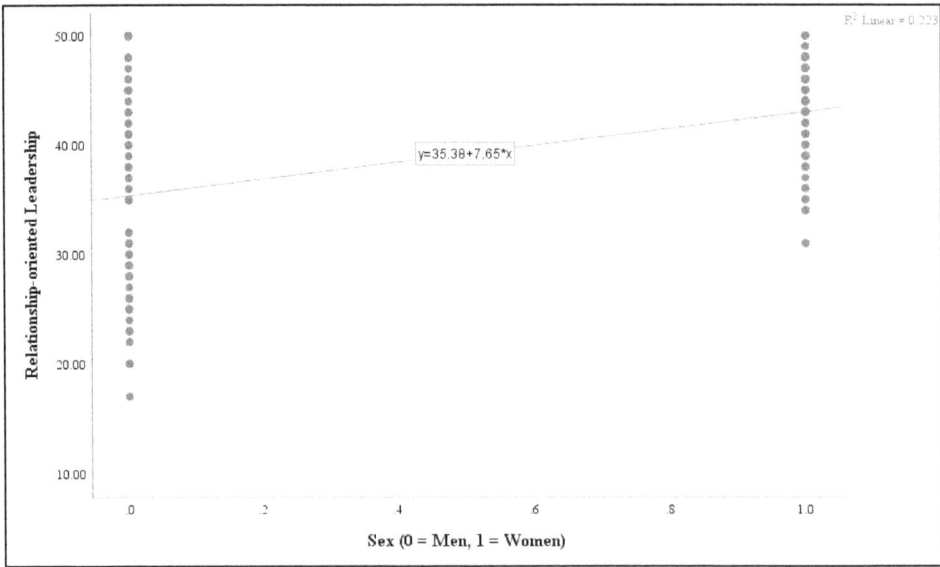

Figure 12. Scatter plot of relationship-oriented leadership and the predictor variable of sex.

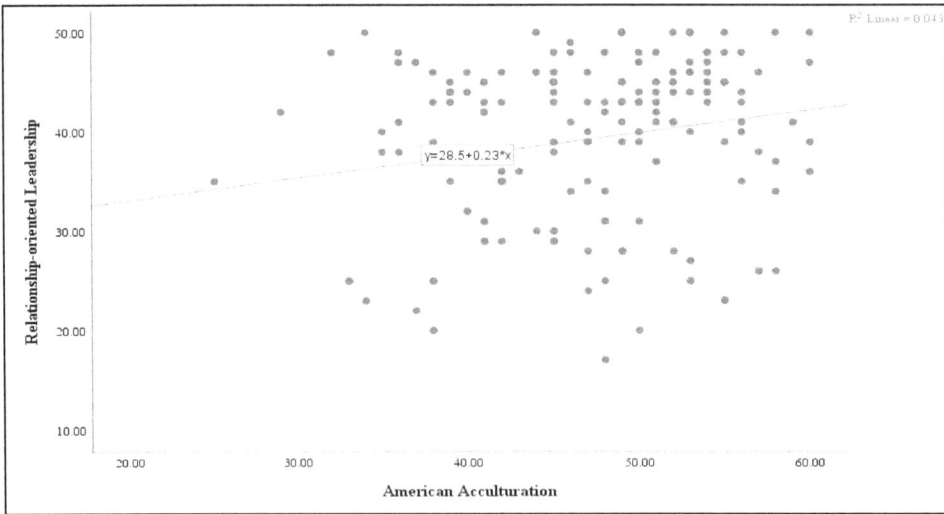

Figure 13. Scatter plot of relationship-oriented leadership and the predictor variable of American acculturation.

The model was re-specified without generation and years of nursing experience. The procedure yielded two separate regression lines that predicted relationship-oriented leadership, one for each group of men and women, respectively:

1. Men predicted relationship-oriented leadership score = 0.53 + 0.44(Afghan acculturation) + 0.39(American acculturation).

2. Women predicted relationship-oriented leadership score = 0.53 + 0.44(Afghan acculturation) + 6.13(sex) + 0.39(American acculturation).

Figure 14 illustrates relationship-oriented leadership means across men and women for each generation. Means on the right side of the graph show that women of both generations showed significantly higher relationship-oriented leadership scores (Gen Y women, $M = 43.46$, $SD = 4.24$, $n = 63$; Gen X women, $M = 41.92$, $SD = 4.51$, $n = 24$) than their male generational counterparts (Gen Y men, $M = 37.63$, $SD = 9.09$, $n = 36$; Gen X men, $M = 33.68$, $SD = 9.07$, $n = 48$). The dotted line shows that Gen Y participants showed relationship-oriented leadership more frequently than did Gen X participants.

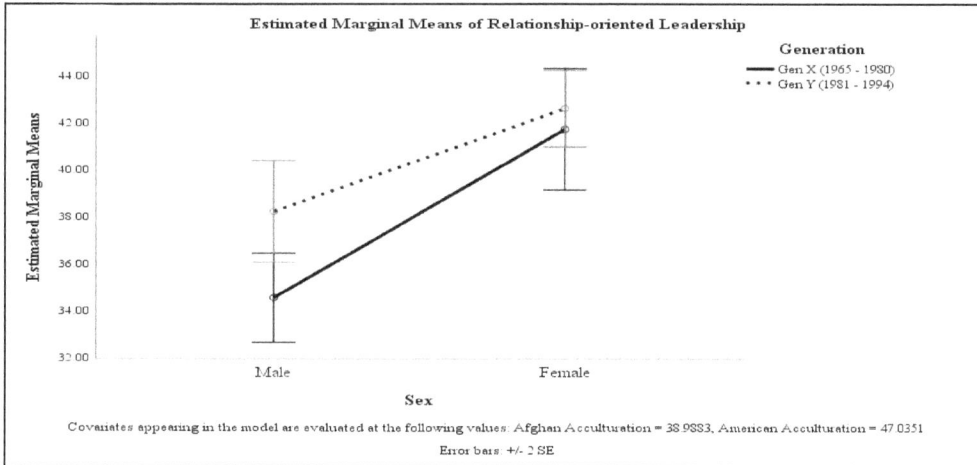

Figure 14. Means of relationship-oriented leadership by generation and sex.

A post hoc power analysis was run on relationship-oriented leadership to measure the power of the regression to avoid a Type II error with GPower software. For the two-tailed test, holding the effect size $R^2 = .42$, $\alpha = .05$, $n = 171$, and three predictors constant, the observed power was $(1 - \beta = 1.00)$.

Answer to RQ4. Relationship-oriented leadership was predicted by a combination of acculturation and participant sex. Both Afghan and American acculturation levels were significant predictors for both men and women with higher scores corresponding to more frequent relationship-oriented leadership, despite the fact that Afghan acculturation and American acculturation were inversely correlated to one another (Table 12). For participant sex, women reported more frequent relationship-oriented leadership than men regardless of generation. Nursing experience and generation were non-significant predictors.

Evaluation of Findings

The evaluation section briefly interprets the study results in light of the existing research and theoretical framework with a more detailed discussion in Chapter V. The results of this study were consistent with existing research and theory. Specifically, the leadership literature shows that men from certain cultures, including Russian, German, and Filipino, are often more likely to exhibit higher levels of task-oriented leadership than are women (Nguyen et al., 2012; Nguyen et al., 2015; Mujtaba & Balboa, 2009). Results of the current study confirmed that men were more task-oriented (RQ1 and RQ2) and women were more relationship-oriented (RQ3 and RQ4). The noteworthy and expected results of this study on Afghan American registered nurses based on the literature include:

1. Afghan American women had higher relationship-oriented leadership scores, which corroborates the findings of Mujtaba and Sadat (2010). The findings showed that Afghan female expatriates (mainly from the US) had a relationship-oriented mean of 43.9 while Afghan male expatriates had a task-oriented mean of 41.26. Furthermore, higher levels of

American and Afghan acculturation were associated with higher levels of relationship-oriented leadership. Mujtaba and Sadat (2010) showed that local and expatriate female Afghans had overall higher relationship-oriented scores ($M = 43.75$) when compared to local and expatriate task-oriented scores ($M = 41.24$). Mujtaba and Sadat (2010) stated that the overall trend was that Afghans have a higher score on the relationship orientation ($M = 43.75$) when compared to task orientation ($M = 41.24$). Mujtaba and Alsua (2011) concluded that American working adults and business students from Alaska and Florida have significantly higher scores on relationship-oriented ($M = 41.98$) when compared to task-orientation ($M = 37.63$).

2. The strongest statistically significant correlation of this study involving task-oriented leadership of men reporting more frequent task-oriented leadership than women corroborates the findings of Manganaro and Alozie (2011).

3. The correlation between years of nursing experience and sex indicated that men tend to have somewhat more nursing experience and were also more task-oriented which confirms the findings of Hoodfar (2007), Aseel (2003), and Aslami (2011).

4. Afghan American women are more relationship-oriented regardless of culture and generation. Possibly, this is because Afghan women are conditioned to focus more on building and maintaining relationships both inside and outside of the house which corroborates the findings of several studies (Aseel, 2003; Aslami, 2011; Hoodfar, 2007).

5. Afghan American millennials (Gen Y) were more Americanized than were Gen X participants. Given that the first generation of Afghans migrated to the US during the Afghan-Russian war (1979-1989), this corroborates the findings of Stempel et al. (2017) and Aseel (2003), and more importantly, the millennials were born outside of Afghanistan due to the war.

6.   The difference in American acculturation between Gen Y participants and Gen X participants was statistically different; Gen Y participants were more Americanized than were Gen X participants.

One unexpected finding was that the more Americanized the participant, regardless of sex, the less task-oriented they tended to be. One potential explanation for this finding may be that Afghan American male nurses who are more Americanized understand and see the value of being relationship-oriented when assisting patients. If that explanation is correct, it would corroborate the study by Arnold et al. (2014), in which care providers in Kabul, Afghanistan were not satisfied with their jobs because they were trained to be task-oriented, and as a result, were overwhelmed with high patient numbers and long hours which negatively impacted patient care.

Summary

A total of 171 Afghan American nurses completed the survey of this study. The results confirmed that men were more task-oriented (RQ1 and RQ2) and women were more relationship-oriented (RQ3 and RQ4). Task-oriented leadership correlated significantly with American acculturation, years of nursing experience, and participant sex. Task-oriented leadership was predicted by the male sex, followed by years of nursing experience, generation, and Afghan acculturation. Relationship-oriented leadership correlated significantly with all five predictor variables (American acculturation, Afghan acculturation, generation, nursing experience, and participant sex). Relationship-oriented leadership was predicted by acculturation and sex.

Chapter V: Discussion and Conclusions

Afghan American registered nurses in this study were surveyed using the Leadership Style Questionnaire (LSQ) to learn about their leadership styles and propensities due to traditional customs and norms. Study participants were also surveyed using the Acculturation Rating Scale (ARS) to determine the extent of acculturation to American customs and norms. The variables of interest to this study were *sex*, *generational affiliation*, *nursing experience*, and *acculturation level*. Results of the analysis confirmed that male participants were more task-oriented (RQ1 and RQ2) and female participants were more relationship-oriented (RQ3 and RQ4). Best practices for the ethical treatment of research participants was adhered to by ensuring that participants understood the purpose of this study and understood their rights as participants. A brief synopsis of the results includes:

1. Task-oriented leadership correlated significantly with American acculturation ($r = -.44$) years of nursing experience ($r = .21$), and participant sex ($r = -.18$).
2. Relationship-oriented leadership correlated significantly with all five potential predictor variables, which were American acculturation ($r = .21$), Afghan acculturation ($r = .32$), generation ($r = .30$), nursing experience ($r = -.33$), and participant sex ($r = .47$).

The results in layman's terms:

Task-oriented leadership as most strongly predicted by sex, and specifically men. Men were significantly more task-oriented than were women. In addition, because Gen X men were more closely associated with longer nursing experience and higher levels of Afghan acculturation, these predictor variables also made significant contributions to predicting task-oriented leadership.

1. Relationship-oriented leadership was predicted by a combination of acculturation and participant sex. Both Afghan and American acculturation levels were significant predictors for both men and women with higher scores corresponding to more frequent relationship-oriented leadership, despite the fact that Afghan acculturation and American acculturation were inversely correlated to one another. For participant sex, women reported more frequent relationship-oriented leadership than men regardless of generation. Nursing experience and generation were non-significant predictors.

Moreover, the following results were expected given the literature:

1. Afghan American women had higher relationship-oriented leadership scores and higher levels of both Afghan acculturation and American acculturation, which corroborated the findings of Aseel (2003), Aslami (2011), Hoodfar (2007), and Manganaro and Alozie (2011). For example, Manganaro and Alozie (2011) concluded that Afghanistan had strict gender rules where each gender has his or her own place. Aslami (2011) discussed how the roles for men, women, and children were clearly outlined in the Afghan culture and were not to be compromised. Women are mainly homemakers and do the child rearing while fathers control the household and make all the important decisions. Talwar (2014) stated that, "migration to the US can provide exposure to a radically different society. For men too, the social expectations regarding protecting women and families could alter when they are no longer in a sociopolitical context that enforces a hierarchical relationship between men and women" (p. 34). Mujtaba and Sadat (2010) noted that the overall trend was that Afghans have a higher score on the relationship orientation when compared to task orientation. Mujtaba and Alsua (2011) concluded that American working adults

90

and business students from Alaska and Florida had significantly higher scores on being relationship-oriented when compared to being task-orientation.

2. The strongest statistically significant correlation involving task-oriented leadership was that men reported more frequent task-oriented leadership than did women, which corroborated the findings of Aseel (2003), Aslami (2011), Hoodfar (2007), and Manganaro and Alozie (2011). For example, Hoodfar (2007) discussed how the schools generally requested help from student fathers for renovations and improvements to classrooms and schools, which accorded with traditional gender roles and expertise. Teachers generally preferred to involve mothers around issues of student well-being and academic performance. Aseel (2003) discussed how men were the breadwinners and women were the caretakers.

3. The correlation between years of nursing experience and sex indicates that men tended to have somewhat more nursing experience and were also more task-oriented, which corroborated the findings of Aseel (2003), Aslami (2011), Hoodfar (2007), and Manganaro and Alozie (2011). For example, Aslami (2011) explained how boys had more educational opportunities because they were expected to be the head of the households and educating women was not and remains unnecessary. The point may explain why Afghan males have more nursing experience.

4. Afghan American women are more relationship-oriented regardless of culture and generation, which corroborates the findings of several studies Aseel (2003), Aslami (2011), Hoodfar (2007), and Manganaro and Alozie (2011).

5. Afghan American millennial participants (Gen Y) were more Americanized. It should be mentioned that the first generation of Afghans migrated to the US during the Afghan-Russian war (1979-1989) and many millennials were born on the way to or in the US (Aseel, 2003; Stempel et al., 2017).

6. There was a statistically significant difference in American acculturation between Gen X participants and Gen Y participants. Gen Y participants were more Americanized than were Gen X participants, which corroborated the findings on Chinese immigrants by Xu et al. (2018) and Iranian immigrants by Hormozi et al. (2018).

Implications

When entering the US, immigrants bring unique traditions, cultures, and customs. According to Ludwick and Silva (2000), certainly members of any culture may hold varying degrees of commitment to the predominant values of the culture but being in opposition to those values sets the stage for conflict. Talwar (2014) stated that maintaining heritage culture provides pathways to belonging to the ethno-cultural groups within which they are more likely to be accepted.

Acculturation is one of the frequently used variables in career development research because of its significance to many aspects of career development for immigrants. According to Miller and Kerlow-Myers (2009), acculturation has been linked to a number of important career outcomes such as job choice and satisfaction, performance reviews, career decision self-efficacy, and occupational stress. Tang (2019) explained that low acculturated individuals might experience more struggles in career development because they try to fulfill their roles in a society with different values and expectations than their traditions. The author further states that acculturation is an important factor for the career development of immigrants and minority members and needs to be considered for its impact on career. The current dissertation study answered four important research questions regarding Afghan American registered nurses.

Predictors of Leadership Style

The role of sex, generation, experience, and acculturation is important because they have the potential to influence leadership style. For example, the Iron Cloud (2019) study on the Oglala Lakota people showed that qualitative themes revealed leadership values similar to servant leadership among all respondents regardless of acculturation level. Harrington et al. (2013) found that leadership style does vary considerably by cultural attributes of pharmacist preceptors.

Moreover, the Dale (2010) study of Latino leaders confirmed a positive association between acculturation level and leadership style. Mujtaba and Sadat (2010) showed that Afghan expatriate males were more task-oriented and Afghan females were more relationship-oriented. According to Talwar (2014), exploring gender among Afghan immigrants in the US provides an opportunity to see how the Afghan people may have tried to construct and understand gender when they were able to distance themselves from Afghanistan, which fostered rigid ideas of gender. Such points are imperative to this study because as Barnes (2017) explained, with the majority of senior American leaders in the present-day workforce still being male and from the baby boomer generation, the values, leadership style, and mindsets are significantly different from millennial women. Talwar (2014) explained that the Afghan American acculturation process revealed an awareness of the differences and similarities between the Afghan and US culture.

The Afghan culture values masculine traits such as decisiveness and assertiveness, but more importantly, males and females have specific gender roles. Ahmadzai (2014) provided an example of this by stating that healthcare decisions are typically made by the male members in the family. Aslami (2011) further clarified how Afghan American girls were at a disadvantage when it came to education due to cultural values. Males are expected

93

to obtain an education and find employment so they are able to pay for all the family expenses, which may explain why task-oriented leadership correlated significantly with American acculturation, years of nursing experience, and participant sex. Crites et al. (2015) explained that in the American workforce men are generally perceived as doers (i.e., task-oriented) and achievers whereas women are thought to have better interpersonal skills (i.e., relationship-oriented) than men and to have more passive qualities. As such, this may explain why Afghan males, with higher American acculturation scores, and with more years of work experience, are more task oriented. Both the American and Afghan culture expect males to be more task oriented. In this study, Gen X men had longer nursing experience than Gen Y, which is understandable because they are older. Gen Y men were as strongly task oriented as Gen X men, which is understandable because the participants were Afghans and felt closely associated with the Afghan culture.

The results of this present study also suggested that the Afghan American millennials (Gen Y) were more Americanized. The first generation of Afghans migrated to the US during the Afghan-Russian war (1979-1989) (Aseel, 2003; Stempel et al., 2017). The migration can be explained because the Gen X participants in this study were born and raised in Afghanistan before the war and the millennials were born outside of Afghanistan. Furthermore, Gen Y males in this study were more relationship-oriented than their Gen X counterparts, which can perhaps be explained by living, working, socializing, and learning from the contemporary lax American culture.

The higher a participant's relationship-oriented score, the higher their Afghan acculturation score and American acculturation score, the higher the likelihood that they were Gen Y and were women. The result confirms the findings of Manganaro and Alozie (2011), who concluded that Afghanistan had strict gender rules in that each gender had his or her own place. According to a World Bank (2005) report about Afghan women, women

94

not only carry the burden of symbolizing the honor of the family but are often seen as embodying the national honor as well. The point may suggest that first-generation Afghan American females were raised in a household in which their fathers were more task-oriented and mothers were more relationship-oriented which may have influenced their upbringing, values, and dominant leadership style.

Relationship-oriented leadership was predicted by sex and acculturation. Specifically, females showed more relationship-oriented leadership than did males. Generally, Afghan American females are more relationship-oriented regardless of culture and generation because, according to the Afghan culture, they are conditioned to focus more on building and maintaining relationships both inside and outside of the house which confirmed the findings of several studies (Aseel, 2003; Aslami, 2011; Hoodfar, 2007). Higher levels of both American acculturation and Afghan acculturation were associated with higher levels of relationship-oriented leadership. Mujtaba and Sadat (2010) concluded that the overall trend was that Afghans had a higher score on the relationship orientation when compared to task orientation. Moreover, Mujtaba and Alsua (2011) also concluded that American working adults and business students had higher scores on being relationship-oriented when compared to being task-orientated. Thus, this may explain a similarity between both cultures and an easier transition to the acculturating process.

As discussed in the Literature Search Strategy in Chapter II, an extensive search in a number of databases identified no published works on leadership style of Afghan American registered nurses working in the US healthcare system. As such, this study contributes to the literature on Afghan Americans and, more specifically, on acculturation and the leadership style of Afghan American nurses working in the US health system. The study may potentially help prevent obstacles and barriers for Afghan American nurses seeking promotions, administrative positions, or career advancement working in the US healthcare system by raising individual awareness of their own leadership styles (Aseel, 2003; Heggertveit-Aoudia, 2012). By evaluating and understanding their own leadership style and also how others perceive their leadership style, Afghan American nurses can consider how they may benefit from using a more comprehensive approach contingent upon each and every situation. According to Kumar and Khiljee (2015), there are nine components of an effective healthcare leader that mainly focus on both relationship and task skills.

The main contribution to the field of healthcare administration is that culture can influence the leadership style of registered nurses, and as a result, healthcare systems should invest in leadership development trainings for nurses due to the high demand of healthcare administrators needed by 2026 (Bureau of Labor Statistics, 2018; Dunne et al., 2015). Sonnino (2016) mentioned that training in the multifaceted components of leadership is now accepted as highly desirable for health care leaders. Despite natural leadership instincts, some core leadership competencies must be formally taught or refined for maximizing leadership effectiveness. According to Ojemeni et al. (2019), as leaders, nurses are the centerpiece of healthcare, making sure processes are functioning to meet the needs of patients. In addition, nurses directly and indirectly oversee all facets of care and are vital contributors to healthcare delivery. Dunne et al. (2015) explained that effective nursing leadership led to higher functioning organizations and improved patient outcomes.

Study Strengths

The present study has several strengths that will be discussed. The empirical research was a non-experimental, descriptive, quantitative correlational study that used primary retrospective data to investigate the complex issues of predicting leadership style. The sample size was large enough to generalize to other Afghan Americans working in different fields in the public or private sectors. The population (i.e., registered nurses) was narrow, which helped with reliability and validity issues.

Limitations

Limitations of the current study include Afghan American nurse willingness to participate and lack of external verification that each participant was a nurse of Afghan descent. Limitations further include potential exposure to unique healthcare experiences that affected a personal leadership style or willingness to disclose personal leadership style honestly. For example, a participant with a dominant task-oriented leadership style could have made past decisions that led to a negative patient outcome and subsequently, that participant changed their leadership style to a relationship orientation as a result. Such information was not solicited. In addition, this study recruited a sample of participants who provided self-report data. Self-reported data are artificial to some extent in that they do not measure participant behavior directly in the typical environment where it occurs (Gliner & Morgan, 2000). Participant awareness that they are 'being studied' also frequently influences self-reported data (Gliner & Morgan, 2000). Participant awareness easily invokes the social desirability bias, which engenders participant intrinsic desire to appear socially acceptable to researchers despite assurances of anonymity (Gliner & Morgan, 2000). The social desirability bias seems likely to be relevant to leadership behavior in the healthcare setting because of social pressure among medical professionals to present subject matter expertise because lives are at stake. According to Dalton et al. (2011), "when self-reported data is used, the social desirability response bias can moderate, attenuate, or inflate the relationship between predictor and criterion variables" (p. 75). Given the sensitivity about lawsuits in healthcare, another limitation is that healthcare workers may feel tempted to cover for something, such as the true quality of their manner at work or what they may believe to be their own leadership shortcomings. However, to limit confidentiality and social desirability bias, no researcher was not present while the participants completed the surveys and survey questions were formulated and presented in a neutral manner (Krumpal, 2013).

Potential Bias and Confounding Factors

A potential bias was that the principal research of the study shares the same nationality as the participants being studied, which may have influenced the results in unknown ways. A possible confounding variable was the intensity or extent of the devotion at home to the Afghan culture. A family who really focused on keeping their core beliefs and traditions alive may have had a different impact on developing children than a family who embraced American ways as the new lifestyle.

Delimitations

One delimitation of this study was the sole inclusion of nurses of Afghan descent working in direct patient care in the US healthcare system. Therefore, the results may not be generalizable to all Afghans or other industries. By focusing on Afghan Gen X and Gen Y nurses, Afghan baby boomers were excluded. Another delimitation was that this research only examined task and relationship-oriented leadership styles based upon the Leadership Style Questionnaire.

Recommendations

Based upon the findings of this study, leadership development training at the community level is recommended to help Afghan American males and females have a more balanced task- and relationship-oriented leadership style that coincide with the nine components of an effective healthcare leader that mainly focus on relationship and task skills identified by Kumar and Khiljee (2015). Similarly, these training sessions should be conducted for other cultures and nationalities. Being able to emphasize the importance of both leadership styles may help Afghan Americans reflect upon and develop their leadership skills.

Based upon the findings of this study such as distinct sex differences in leadership style, the difference in American acculturation between Gen X and Gen Y was statistically significant, which means that Gen Y participants were more Americanized than were Gen X participants. Additionally, the more relationship-oriented leadership a participant reported, the less experience they had in the nursing profession. Senior administrators in the US healthcare system should consider focusing on leadership development trainings for nurses so they can consider the benefits of using a more balanced leadership style that encompasses the Healthcare Leadership Alliance (HLA) model, which emphasizes five competency domains that relate to being both task-oriented and relationship-oriented. According to Ojemeni et al. (2019), nurses are best positioned to make a healthcare system stronger because they know their patients best (i.e., they are the closest to the patient). Collins and Holton (2004) conducted a meta-analysis of 83 studies involving leadership interventions and found that leadership development programs could lead to significant improvements in knowledge and skills but only when adequate preparation for such interventions had taken place beforehand. Formal nursing leadership education in the United States is available through graduate education and professional nursing organization programs (West et al., 2016). As such, most RNs without a graduate level degree are not exposed to advanced training in leadership unless their employers provide or sponsor the training or if they participate in continuing education courses to maintain their licenses.

Leadership is a process that takes time and dedication. United States health systems should consider providing leadership trainings to all nurses. However, simply providing leadership training for staff does not in itself lead to such results; training programs must be based on an initial needs assessment that reflects both the needs of the organization and the individual needs of the participants.

Application of Findings

According to Kapp et al. (2015), findings from scientific research unfortunately remain inside the scientific community and more importantly, research scientists are being encouraged to use social media for dissemination of evidence. The findings of this research study will be applied to help prepare nurse leaders for the increased demand for healthcare administrators because of the aging US population. The first approach is to communicate the findings in a clear and concise manner by using social media. Some other potential venues where the research findings will be shared are: (a) community conferences known for strengthening the diaspora, (b) non-profit organizations that focus on empowering refugee families, and (c) the creation of an informational website as a result of this research study. Another avenue for this research to help in an applied manner includes providing resources to help (i.e., pro-bono) all nurses (on a more global level) to reflect upon and develop their leadership skills given the study by Arnold et al. (2018) that noted social expectations and political pressures influenced decision-making and the quality of care as Afghan healthcare providers were confronted daily with the clash between world-views and values. Lastly, to reach a larger number of nurses and administrators, the findings of this research study will be presented online and at different national nursing conferences.

Future Research

As the first study focusing on Afghan American registered nurses, future researchers should consider a mixed-methods study for triangulation purposes. According to Halcomb and Andrew (2005), a major focus of nursing research is to provide evidence upon which to base clinical nursing practice. Clinical nurses rely upon evidence to reflect the reality of nursing. Triangulation has the ability to inform nursing research in such a way as to be valuable in guiding nursing practice. Future researchers can consider comparing Licensed Vocational Nurses (LVNs or LPNs) to Registered Nurses (RNs) to Nurse Practitioners (NPs) to see if there are significant differences among the groups. Also, it would be interesting to evaluate nurses in formal leadership roles. A larger sample size can also be beneficial. The next logical step for research to use a qualitative method to interview healthcare senior administrators to learn more about their visions, specific needs, and leadership expectations of nurses. Future researchers should consider a longitudinal study that involves comparing first and second-generation Afghan American nurses. Furthermore, future researchers should consider comparing American nurses with Afghan American nurses among similar nursing settings and with similar job titles. Lastly, the same survey should be used on other first-generation Americans to learn more about how acculturation factors impact their leadership style.

Conclusions

In current demanding healthcare environment, identifying and developing nursing leaders is one of the greatest challenges faced by the nursing profession (Scully, 2015). The field of nursing was traditionally a female-dominated profession but has flourished into a gender-neutral and highly in-demand field. The findings of this study corroborate a number of different studies (Aseel, 2003; Aslami, 2011; Hoodfar, 2007; Mujtaba & Balboa, 2009;

101

Mujtaba & Sadat, 2010; Nguyen et al., 2012; Nguyen et al., 2015). According to Cowsill and Grint (2008), leaders that over-focus on building relationships without a purpose or over-focus on securing task completion at the expense of concerns for followers are unlikely to succeed. Mujtaba (2009) explained that effective leaders stay in control by managing through a balance of both task- and relationship-oriented behaviors, as appropriate, to make sure the objectives and goals are accomplished. Begum and Mujtaba (2016) stressed the importance of effective leaders being flexible enough to accommodate the contextual demands in their style to maintain a healthy balance without compromising on the objectives or relations of organization. According to Wise (2019), health systems require leaders with excellent relational skills but who are also clever with finances and procedures, particularly at the senior and executive nurse management levels where many decisions around the implementation of new managerial policies and procedures are made. Ojemeni et al. (2019) noted that it is essential for nurses to not only be embedded into groups but rather to be at the forefront of leadership teams to develop solutions given their unique perspective that best represents patient needs.

For Afghan Americans who would like to work in Afghanistan and assist with the development process as an expatriate, it is important to mention that he or she may initially deal with culture shock from a leadership and human resource management perspective and then may deal with reverse culture shock once they repatriate (Chiang et al., 2018).

Due to the constantly changing nursing field and high demand for healthcare administrators, nursing curriculum should emphasize the importance of leadership skills. Hospitals should consider implementing more training courses and opportunities for nurses to develop their leadership skills. According to West et al. (2016), succession planning requires a constant competitive pool of qualified nursing leader candidates and retention of those interested in career growth. Effective mentoring programs and succession plans can help develop the next generation of diverse nursing leaders.

References

American Association of Nurse Practitioners. (2019). What's a nurse practitioner? *American Association of Nurse Practitioners*. https://www.aanp.org/about/all-about-nps/whats-a-nurse-practitioner

Abbasi-Shavazi, M. J., & Sadeghi, R. (2015). Socio-cultural adaptation of second-generation Afghans in Iran. *International Migration*, *53*(6), 89-110. doi:10.1111/imig.12148

Abraído-Lanza, A., Armbrister, A., Flórez, K., & Aguirre, A. (2006). Toward a theory-driven model of acculturation in public health research. *American Journal of Public Health*, *96*(8), 1342–1346.

Aghamirza, N. (2015). *An examination of acculturation levels and evaluation of leadership knowledge and experiences of first-generation immigrant leaders at the district offices and school sites in the mid-Atlantic region of the United States* (Order No. 3734345).

Al Anezi, A., & Al Ansari, B. (2016). Gender differences in Hofstede's cultural dimensions among a Kuwaiti sample. *European Psychiatry*, *33*, 503-504.

American Association of Colleges of Nursing (AACN). (2008). The essentials of baccalaureate education for professional nursing practice. *American Association of Colleges of Nursing*. http://www.aacn.nche.edu/education-resources/BaccEssentials08.pdf

Anderson, D. (2016). Servant leadership, emotional intelligence: Essential for baccalaureate nursing students. *Creative Nursing, 22*(3), 176-180.

Arnold, V., Teijlingen, E., Ryan, K., & Holloway, I. (2014). Understanding Afghan healthcare providers: A qualitative study of the culture of care in a Kabul maternity hospital. *BJOG – An International Journal of Obstetrics and Gynecology, 122*, 260–267.

Arnold, V., Teijlingen, E., Ryan, K., & Holloway, I. (2018). Parallel worlds: An ethnography of care in an Afghan maternity hospital. *Social Science & Medicine*, *216*, 33-40.

Aseel, M. Q. (2003). *Torn between two cultures*. Capital Books Inc.: Herndon, VA.

Aslami, W. (2011). *Afghan immigrant parents with daughters seeking to attend college away from home: Adlerian group counseling for parents and daughters* (Order No. 1501366). ProQuest Dissertations & Theses Global.

Azizi, M. (2008). *Leaders of higher education in Afghanistan: Leadership beliefs and challenges for the 21st century* (Order No. 3336791). ProQuest Dissertations & Theses Global. (304825477).

Barnes, E. (2016). *A qualitative study on the impact of a transformational leadership educational intervention within healthcare organizations* (Order No. 10149707). ProQuest Dissertations & Theses Global. (1832304439).

Barnes, J. (2017). Climbing the stairs to leadership: Reflections on moving beyond the stained-glass ceiling. *Journal of Leadership Studies*, 10(4), 47–53.

Bass, B. M., & Riggio, R. E. (2006). *Transformational leadership*. Mahwah, NJ: Erlbaum.

Begum, R., & Mujtaba, B. G. (2016). Task and relationship orientation of Pakistani managers and working professionals: The interaction effect of demographics in a collective culture. *Public Organization Review, 16*(2), 199-215.

Bennis, W., & Nanus, B. (2003*). Leaders: Strategies for taking charge* (2nd ed.). New York, United States of America: Harper & Row.

Benton, D., & Shaffer, F. (2016). How the nursing profession can contribute to sustainable development goals. *Nursing Management*, *23*(7), 29-34.

Blais, N. (2019). I am because we are: Awakening revolutionary patient-centered care. *Journal of Emergency Nursing*, *45*(2), 211-213.

Blake, R. R., & Mouton, J. S. (1966). Managerial facades. *Advanced Management Journal*, *31*(3), 30–37.

Bondclegg, M. (2017). *The potential influence of YouTube as a means of disseminating the findings of research to millennial-aged teachers* (Order No. 10263009). ProQuest One Academic. (1882291622).

Bosiok, D., & Novi Sad, S. (2013). Leadership styles and creativity. *Online Journal of Applied Knowledge Management*, *1*(2), 64-77.

Bombuwela, P. M., & De Alwis, A. C. (2013). Effects of glass ceiling on women career development in private sector organizations-case of Sri Lanka. *Journal of Competitiveness*, *5*(2), 3-19.

Bourne, R. (1916). Trans-national America. *Atlantic Monthly*.

Bullock, G. A. (2015). *Leadership styles of female healthcare executives: Comparison of transformational, transactional, and passive-avoidant leadership styles* (Order No. 3682571). ProQuest Dissertations & Theses Global. (1658144158).

Bureau of Labor Statistics. (2018). Occupational outlook handbook, medical and health services managers. *US Department of Labor*. https://www.bls.gov/ooh/management/medical-and-health-services-managers.htm

Cann, A., & Siegfried W. D. (1990). Gender stereotypes and dimensions of effective leader behavior. *Sex Roles*, *23*, 413–419.

Caplin-Davies, P. (2003). Management and leadership — A dual role in nursing education. *Nurse Education Today*, *23*(1), 3-10.

Carless, S. (1998). Assessing the discriminant validity of transformational leader behavior as measured by the MLQ. *Journal of Occupational and Organizational Psychology*, *71*, 353–358.

Cascardo, D. (2016). Developing skills that turn physicians into strong leaders in a rapidly changing healthcare environment. *The Journal of Medical Practice Management: MPM, 32*(2), 106-109.

Chen, C.C., & Van Velsor, E. (1996). New directions for research and practice in diversity leadership. *Leadership Quarterly*, *7*(2), 285–302.

Chiang, F. F. T., van Esch, E., Birtch, T. A., & Shaffer, M. A. (2018). Repatriation: What do we know and where do we go from here. *International Journal of Human Resource Management*, *29*(1), 188–226.

Christian, M., & Nickelsen, M. (2019). The infrastructure of telecare: Implications for nursing tasks and the nurse-doctor relationship. *Sociology of Health & Illness*, *41*(1), 67-80.

Collard, J., & Reynolds, C. (2005). *Leadership gender and culture in education.* London, England: Open University Press.

Collins, D., & Holton, E. (2004). The effectiveness of managerial leadership development programs: A meta-analysis of studies from 1982-2001. *Human Resource Development Quarterly*, *15*, 217-248.

Colquitt, J., Lepine, J., & Wesson, M. (2011). *Organizational behavior: Improving performance and commitment in the workplace*. New York, NY: McGraw-Hill/Irwin.

Colquitt, J., & Phelan-Zapata, C. (2007). Trends in theory building and theory testing: A five-decade study of the Academy of Management Journal. *Academy of Management Journal*, *50*(6). 1281-1303.

Coomber, B., & Barriball, K. (2007). Impact of job satisfaction components on intent to leave and turnover for hospital-based nurses: A review of the research literature. *International Journal of Nursing*, *44*(2), 297-314.

Cowsill, R., & Grint, K. (2008). Leadership, task and relationship: Orpheus, Prometheus and Janus. *Human Resource Management Journal*, *18*(2), 188-195. doi:10.1111/j.1748-8583.2007.00065.x

Crites, S. N., Dickson, K. E., & Lorenz, A. (2015). Nurturing gender stereotypes in the face of experience: A study of leader gender, leadership style, and satisfaction. *Journal of Organizational Culture, Communications and Conflict, 19*(1), 1-23.

Cronje, J.C. (2011). Using Hofstede's cultural dimensions to interpret cross-cultural blended teaching and learning. *Computers & Education*, *56*(3), 596-603.

Cuéllar, I., Arnold, B., & Maldonado, R. (1995). Acculturation rating scale for Mexican Americans-II: A revision of the original ARSMA scale. *Hispanic Journal of Behavioral Science, 17*(3), 275-304.

Daaleman, T. P., Shea, C. M., Halladay, J., & Reed, D. (2014). A method to determine the impact of patient-centered care interventions in primary care. *Patient education and counseling, 97*(3), 327-331.

Dalton, D., & Ortegren, M. (2011). Gender differences in ethics research: The importance of controlling for the social desirability response bias. *Journal of Business Ethics, 103*(1), 73-93.

Deguchi, M. (2006). *Finding place in America: Acculturation narratives of Japanese women* (Order No. 3209819). ProQuest Dissertations & Theses Global. (305354031).

Delmatoff, J., & Lazarus, I. R. (2014). The most effective leadership style for the new landscape of healthcare. *Journal of Healthcare Management, 59*(4), 245-249.

Doyle, A. (2018). How often do people change jobs? https://www.thebalancecareers.com/how-often-do-people-change-jobs-2060467

Downey, M., Parslow, S., & Smart, M. (2011). The hidden treasure in nursing leadership: Informal leaders. *Journal of Nursing Management, 19*, 517-521.

Dunne, S., Lunn, C., Kirwan, M., Matthews, A., & Condell, S. (2015). Planning and selecting evaluation designs for leadership training: A toolkit for nurse managers and educators. *Journal of Professional Nursing, 31*(6), 475-481.

Dusek, G., Yurova, Y., & Ruppel, C. (2015). Using social media and targeted snowball sampling to survey a hard-to-reach population: A case study. *International Journal of Doctoral Studies, 10*, 279-299.

Edmonstone, J. D. (2017). Escaping the healthcare leadership cul-de-sac. *Leadership in Health Services, 30*(1), 76-91.

Emerson, E. (2007). Facilitating foreign-educated nurses. *The Online Journal of Issues in Nursing, 13*(1), 1-10.

Epstein, R. M., & Street, R. L. (2011). The values and value of patient-centered care. *Annals of Family Medicine*, *9*(2), 100-103.

Fallon, A., Uí Chiardhaa, T., Meaneya, Y., van der Puttena, D., Brennana, M., Uí Chionnab, J., Bradleyc, S., McNicholasa, M., & Smytha, S. (2018). Revisiting task orientated care: Oral histories of former student nurses in Ireland (1960–2001). *Nurse Education in Practice, 29*, 48-52.

Fardellone, C., Musil, C. M., Smith, E., & Click, E. R. (2014). Leadership behaviors of front-line staff nurses. *Journal of Continuing Education in Nursing*, *45*(11), 506-513.

Fedock, B., & Young, E. (2014). Transformational leadership and patient satisfaction: Redefining bedside nurses' roles. *E-Learn: World Conference on E-Learning in Corporate, Government, Healthcare, and Higher Education*. Las Vegas, NV, USA.

Fisher, A. (2005). Holding on to global talent. *Business Week*.

Frogel, E. (2016). *Afghan Jews and their children: A qualitative study exploring the lived experiences and psychological impact of acculturation on first and second generation traditional afghan Jewish immigrants* (Order No. 10133308). ProQuest Dissertations & Theses Global. (1802044976).

Fleishman, E.A. (1953). The description of supervisory behavior. *Journal of Applied Psychology*, *37*, 1-6.

Fletcher, J. K. (2004). The paradox of postheroic leadership: An essay on gender, power, and transformational change. *The Leadership Quarterly*, *15*, 647-661.

Forteza, J. A., & Prieto, J. M. (1994). *Aging and work behavior*. In H. C. Triandis, M. D. Dunnette, & L. M. Hough (Eds.), Handbook of industrial and organizational psychology (2nd ed., Vol. 4, pp. 447–483). Palo Alto, CA: Consulting Psychologists Press.

Frögéli, E., Rudman, A., & Gustavsson, P. (2019). The relationship between task mastery, role clarity, social acceptance, and stress: An intensive longitudinal study with a sample of newly registered nurses. *International Journal of Nursing Studies, 91*, 60-69.

George, L. (1993). Children of immigrants often torn between two cultures: Assimilation as parents continue to bring their families' hopes and expectations to the United States, a complex tension can develop for young new Americans. *Los Angeles Times*. http://articles.latimes.com/1993-11-28/local/me-61948_1_united-states/2

Gliner, J. A., & Morgan, G. A. (2000). *Research methods in applied settings: An integrated approach to design and analysis*. Mahwah, NJ: Erlbaum.

Grandy, G., & Holton, J. (2013). Leadership development needs assessment in healthcare: A collaborative approach. *Leadership & Organization Development Journal, 34*(5), 427-445.

Grimm, J.W. (2010). Effective leadership: Making the difference. *Journal of Emergency Nursing, 36*(1), 74-77.

Grossman, S., & Valiga, T. (2012). *The new leadership challenge — Creating the future of nursing* (4th ed.). Philadelphia, United States of America: FA Davis Company.

Halcomb, E. J., & Andrew, S. (2005). Triangulation as a method for contemporary nursing research. *Nurse Researcher, 13*(2), 71-82.

Hall, D. T. (2002). *Careers in and out of organizations*. Thousand Oaks, CA: Sage Publications.

Happell, B. (2007). Conference presentations: Developing nursing knowledge by disseminating research findings. *Nurse Researcher, 15*(1), 70-77.

Heggertveit-Aoudia, S. (2012). Culture, values and the impact at work. *Diversity Journal*. http://www.diversityjournal.com/9823-culture-values-and-the-impact-at-work/

Hirschman, C. (2013). The contributions of immigrants to American culture. *Daedalus, 142*(3), 1-19.

Hofstede, G. (1984). Cultural dimensions in management and planning. *Asia Pacific Journal of Management, 1*(2), 81–99.

Hofstede, G. (2001). *Cultures Consequences: Comparing values, behaviors, institutions, and organizations across nations*. Thousand Oaks, CA: Sage.

Hoodfar, H. (2007). Women, religion, and the Afghan education movement in Iran. *Journal of Development Studies, 43*(2), 265-293.

Hormozi, T., Miller, M. M., & Banford, A. (2018). First-generation Iranian refugees' acculturation in the United States: A focus on resilience. *Contemporary Family Therapy: An International Journal*, *40*(3), 276–283.

Hosey, G., Rengiil, A., Maddison, R., Agapito, A., Lippwe, K., M.A., Wally, O., Agapito, D., Seremai, J., Primo, S., Luther, X., Ikerdeu, E., & Satterfield, D. (2016). U.S. associated Pacific islands health care teams chart a course for improved health systems: Implementation and evaluation of a non-communicable disease collaborative model. *Journal of Health Care for the Poor and Underserved, 27*(4), 19-38.

Hou, P., Osborn, D. S., & Sampson, J. (2018). Acculturation and career development of international and domestic college students. *The Career Development Quarterly, 66*(4), 344-357.

Howieson, B., & Thiagarajah, T. (2011). What is clinical leadership? A journal-based meta-review. *International Journal of Clinical Leadership*, *17*(1), 7-18.

Hur, W., Kang, S., & Kim, M. (2015). The moderating role of Hofstede's cultural dimensions in the customer-brand relationship in China and India. *Cross Cultural Management, 22*(3), 487-508.

Institute of Medicine. (2010). *The future of nursing: Leading change, advancing health.* Washington, DC: The National Academies Press.

Institute of Medicine. (2013). *Best care at lower cost: The path to continuously learning health care in America.* Washington, DC: The National Academies Press.

Iron Cloud, R. (2019). *Leadership Values and Acculturation among the Oglala Lakota Leadership* (Order No. 22621056). Available from ProQuest One Academic.

Jadalla, A., & Lee, J. (2015). Validation of Arabic and English versions of the ARSMA-II acculturation rating scale. *Journal of Immigrant and Minority Health, 17*(1), 208-216.

Jacobson, W. S., Palus, C. K., & Bowling, C. J. (2009). A woman's touch? Gendered management and performance in state administration. *Journal of Public Administration Research and Theory, 20*, 477-504.

Jennings, C. (2015). Dr. Qayoumi leaves San Jose State for advisory role in Afghanistan. *ABC News.* http://abc7news.com/education/dr-qayoumi-leaves-san-jose-state-for-role-in-afghanistan/941128/

Jimenez, D.E., Gray, H.L., Cucciare, M., Kumbhani, S., Gallagher-Thompson, D. (2010). Using the revised Acculturation Rating Scale for Mexican Americans (ARSMA-II) with older adults. *Hispanic Health Care International, 8*(1), 14-22.

Jones, E. L., & Jones, R. C. (2017). Leadership style and career success of women leaders in nonprofit organizations. *Advancing Women in Leadership, 37*, 37-48.

Judge, T. A., Piccolo, R. F., & Ilies, R. (2004). The forgotten ones? The validity of consideration and initiating structure in leadership research. *Journal of Applied Psychology, 89*(1), 36-51.

Kaifi, B.A. (2009). *A Critical Hermeneutic Approach to Understanding the Experiences of Selected Afghan American Leaders post-9/11 in the Bay Area* (Order No. 825007). ProQuest Dissertations & Theses Global.

Kaifi, B. A. (2010). *Managing your future: An educational guide.* Davie, Florida. ILEAD Academy. ISBN: 978-1-936237-03-6.

Kaifi, B. A., & Mujtaba, B. G. (2010). Transformational leadership of Afghans and Americans: A study of culture, age and gender. *Journal of Service Science and Management, 3*(1), 150-158.

Kapp, J., Hensel, B., & Schnoring, K. (2015). Is Twitter a forum for disseminating research to health policy makers? *Annals of Epidemiology, 25*(12), 883-887.

Karmaliani, R., McFarlane, J., Asad, N., Madhani, F., Hirani, S., Shehzad, S., & Zaidi, A. (2009). Applying community-based participatory research methods to improve maternal and child health in Karachi, Pakistan. *Nursing Outlook, 57*(4), 204-209.

Katz, D., Maccoby, N., and Morse, N. (1950). *Productivity, supervision, and morale in an office situation.* Ann Arbor, MI: Institute for Social Research, University of Michigan.

Kavanaugh, J. K. (1986). *The content of implicit leadership theories: An investigation of achievement orientation, task orientation, and relationships orientation under varied task difficulty and achievement conditions* (Order No. 8629179). ProQuest Dissertations & Theses Global.

Kessler, I., Heron, P., & Dopson, S. (2015). Professionalization and expertise in care work: The hoarding and discarding of tasks in nursing. *Human Resource Management, 54*(5), 737-752.

Khanfar, N., Harrington, C., Alkhateeb, F., & Kaifi, B. (2013). Cultural differences in leadership styles of pharmacist preceptors. *Business and Management Research, 2,* 1-17.

Kheirkhah, S. P. (2003). *Acculturation among Iranian immigrants in America: A phenomenological inquiry* (Order No. 3080419). ProQuest Dissertations & Theses Global. (288097724).

Khlif, H. (2016). Hofstede's cultural dimensions in accounting research: A review. *Meditari Accountancy Research, 24*(4), 545-573.

Kilpatrick, A. O. (2009). The health care leader as humanist. *Journal of Health and Human Services Administration, 31*(4), 451-465.

Kirkman, B. L., Lowe, K. B. & Gibson, C. B., (2006). A quarter century of culture's consequences: A review of empirical research incorporating Hofstede's cultural values framework. *Journal of International Business Studies, 37*(3), 285-320.

Kiwanuka, F., Shayan, S., & Tolulope, A. (2019). Barriers to patient and family-centered care in adult intensive care units: A systematic review. *Nursing Open*, 1-9.

Krumpal, I. (2013). Determinants of social desirability bias in sensitive surveys: A literature review. *Quality and Quantity, 47*(4), 2025-2047.

Kumar, R., & Khiljee, N. (2015). Leadership in healthcare. *Anesthesia and Intensive Care Medicine, 17*(1), 63-65.

Kumar, U., & Rehnamol, P. R. (2017). The political transformation and status of women in Iran: A critical analysis. *Deliberative Research, 33*(1), 1-6.

Lantz, P., & Maryland, P. (2008). Gender and leadership in healthcare administration: 21st century progress and challenge. *Journal of Healthcare Management, 53*(5), 291–303.

Larsson, I. E., & Sahlsten, M. J. M. (2016). The staff nurse clinical leader at the bedside: Swedish registered nurses' perceptions. *Nursing Research and Practice, 1797014*, 1-8.

Leskiw, S., & Singh, P. (2007). Leadership development: Learning from best practices. *Leadership & Organization Development Journal, 28*, 444-464.

Lo, K. D., Waters, R. D., & Christensen, N. (2017). Assessing the applicability of Hofstede's cultural dimensions for global 500 corporations' Facebook profiles and content. *Journal of Communication Management, 21*(1), 51-67.

Lobo, M. L. (2005). Descriptive research is the bench science of nursing. *Western Journal of Nursing Research, 27*(1), 5-6.

Lord, R. G., DeVader, C. L., & Alliger, G. M. (1986). A meta-analysis of the relation between personality traits and leadership perceptions: An application of validity generalization procedures. *Journal of Applied Psychology, 71*, 402-410.

Lu, Y., Samaratunge, R., & Härtel, C. E. J. (2016). Predictors of acculturation attitudes among professional Chinese immigrants in the Australian workplace. *Journal of Management and Organization, 22*(1), 49-67.

Ludwick, R., & Silva, M. (2000). Ethics: Nursing around the world: Cultural values and ethical conflicts. *Online Journal of Issues in Nursing*, *5*(3), 1-10.

Manyak, T. G., & Mujtaba, B. G (2013). Task and relationship orientations of Ugandans and Americans. *International Business and Management*, *6*(1), 12-20.

Mannix, J., Wilkes, L., & Daly, J. (2013). Attributes of clinical leadership in contemporary nursing: An integrative review. *Contemporary Nurse: A Journal for the Australian Nursing Profession*, *45*(1), 10-21.

Marin, G., & Marin, B. (1991). *Research with Hispanic populations*. Newbury Park, CA: Sage.

Markus, H. R. & Kitayama, S., (1991). Culture and the self: Implications for cognition, emotion, and motivation, *Psychological Review*, *98*(2), 224-253.

McKay, D. (2018). How often do people change jobs? *The Balance Careers*. https://www.thebalancecareers.com/how-often-do-people-change-careers-3969407

Mhoon-Walker, E. (2013). *Leadership styles and effectiveness among C-level healthcare executives* (Order No. 3553927). ProQuest Dissertations & Theses Global. (1315239814).

Miller, M. J., & Kerlow-Myers, A. E. (2009). A content analysis of acculturation research in the career development literature. *Journal of Career Development*, *35*(4), 352-384.

Morley, M. (2018). *Task vs. relationship leadership theories. Small Business Chronicle*. http://smallbusiness.chron.com/task-vs-relationship-leadership-theories-35167.html

Morrill, D. (2018). Teaching teamwork and collaboration: A task-centered clinical design. *Nurse Education Today*, *69*, 120-121.

Mujtaba, B. (2010). An examination of Bahamian respondents' task and relationship orientations: Do males have a significantly different score than females? *Journal of Diversity Management*, *5*(3), 35-41.

Mujtaba, B. G., & Isomura, K. (2012). Examining the Japanese leadership orientations and their changes. *Leadership & Organization Development Journal, 33*(4), 401-420.

Mujtaba, B. G., & Balboa, A. (2009). Comparing Filipino and American task and relationship orientations. *Journal of Applied Management and Entrepreneurship, 14*(2), 82-98.

Mujtaba, B. G., & Alsua, C. J. (2011). Task and relationship orientation of Americans: A study of gender, age, and work experience. *Journal of Behavioral Studies in Business, 3*(1), 27-36.

Mujtaba, B. G., Cai, H., Lian, Y., & Ping, H. (2013). Task and relationship orientation of Chinese students and managers in the automotive industry. *Journal of Technology Management in China, 8*(3), 142 – 154.

Mujtaba, B. G. (2013). Ethnic diversity, distrust and corruption in Afghanistan: Reflections on the creation of an inclusive culture. *Equality, Diversity and Inclusion: An International Journal, 32*(3), 245-261.

Mujtaba, B. G., Marschke, E., & Nguyen, L. D. (2012). Leadership orientation and stress Perceptions of American business students. *International Business and Management, 4*(2), 7-15.

Mujtaba, B. G., & Sadat, S. K. (2010). Leadership knowledge of local and expatriate Afghans: Are they leaning more toward tasks or relationships? *Journal of Business Studies Quarterly, 1*(3), 1-12.

Mujtaba, B. G., & Balboa, A. (2009). Comparing Filipino and American task and relationship orientations. *Journal of Applied Management and Entrepreneurship, 14*(2), 82-98.

Mujtaba, B. G., & Kaifi, B. A. (2010). An inquiry into eastern leadership orientation of working adults in Afghanistan. *Journal of Leadership Studies, 4*(1), 36-46.

Mujtaba, B. G., Khanfar, N. M., & Khanfar, S. M. (2010). Leadership tendencies of government employees in Oman: A study of task and relationship based on age and gender. *Public Organization Review, 10*(2), 173-190. doi: 10.1007/s11115-009-0103-x

National Health Service Leadership Academy. (2013). *Healthcare leadership model: The nine dimensions of leadership* (Vers. 1.0). National Health Service.

Ndika, N. (2013). Acculturation: A pilot study on Nigerians in America and their coping strategies. *SAGE Open*, 1-8.

Negron, M. (2012). *Analysis of servant leadership: An interpretive biography of a prominent leader in proprietary higher education* (Order No. 3506701). ProQuest Dissertations & Theses Global. (1018566761).

Nguyen, L. D., Mujtaba, B. G., & Ruijs, A. (2014). Stress, task, and relationship orientations of Dutch: Do age, gender, education, and government work experience make a difference? *Public Organization Review, 14*(3), 305-324.

Nguyen, L. D., & Mujtaba, B. G. (2011). Stress, task, and relationship orientations of Vietnamese: An examination of gender, age and government work experience in the Asian culture. *Competition Forum, 9*(2), 235-246.

Nguyen, L. D., Mujtaba, B. G., & Ruijs, A. (2014). Stress, task, and relationship orientations of Dutch: Do age, gender, education, and government work experience make a difference? *Public Organization Review, 14*(3), 305-324.

Nguyen, L. D., & Mujtaba, B. G. (2011). Stress, task, and relationship orientations of Vietnamese: An examination of gender, age, and government work experience in the Asian culture. *Competition Forum, 9*(2), 235-246.

Nguyen, L. D., Mujtaba, B. G., & Boehmer, T. (2012). Stress, task, and relationship orientations across German and Vietnamese Cultures. *International Business and Management, 5*(1), 10-20.

Nguyen, L. D., Mujtaba, B. G., Tran, Q. H. M, & Tran, C. N. (2014). Do age and management experience make a difference in leadership orientations? An empirical study of Omani and Vietnamese working adults. *Academy of Business Disciplines Journal, 6*(1), 1-16.

Nguyen, L. D., Lee, K., Mujtaba, B. G., Ruijs, A., & Boehmer, T. (2012). Stress, task, and relationship orientations across German and Dutch cultures. *International Journal of Business and Applied Sciences*, *1*(1), 30-46.

Nguyen, L. D., Ermasova, N., Geyfman, V., & Mujtaba, B. G. (2015). Leadership orientations of Russian working adults: Do age, gender, education, and government work experience make a difference? *Public Organization Review, 15*(3), 399-413.

Northouse, P. (2004). *Leadership: Theory and practice* (3rd edition). Thousand Oaks, CA: SAGE Publications.

Ojemeni, M., Karanja, V., Cadet, G., Charles, A., Abbasi, S., McMahon, C., & Davis, S. (2019). Fostering nursing leadership: An important key to achieving sustainable development goals and universal health care. *International Journal of Nursing Studies*, *100*, 1-2.

Oudenhoven, J. P., & Ward, C. (2013). Fading majority cultures: The implications of transnationalism and demographic changes for immigrant acculturation. *Journal of Community & Applied Social Psychology*, *23*(2), 81-97. doi:10.1002/casp.2132

Park, R. E., & Burgess, E. W. (1921). *Introduction to the science of society.* Chicago, IL: University of Chicago Press.

Paris, T. D. J. (2003). *Acculturation, assimilation, leadership styles and its consequences on job satisfaction* (Order No. 3088536). ProQuest Dissertations & Theses Global. (305216527).

Pielstick, C. D. (2000). Formal vs. informal leading: A comparative analysis. *Journal of Leadership and Organizational Studies*, *7*(3), 99-114.

Politis, J. D., Politis, D. J., & Politis, N. J. (2018). *Initiating structure and consideration leadership – creativity and innovation relationships: The Cypriot and the United Arab Emirates experience. Proceedings of the European Conference on Management, Leadership & Governance*, 213-220.

Pounder, J. S., & Coleman, M. (2002). Women—Better leaders than men? In general and educational management, it still "all depends." *Leadership & Organization Development Journal, 23*(3), 122-133.

Qarani, W. M., Rafat, J., Saeed, K. M. I., & Khymani, L. (2018). We need higher education: Voice of nursing administration from Kabul, Afghanistan. *Nursing Open, 5*(3), 317-322.

Quinones, M. A., Ford, J. K., & Teachout, M. S. (1995). The relationship between work experience and job performance: A conceptual and meta-analytic review. *Personnel Psychology, 48*, 887–910.

Rahmani, A. I. (2016). *Political leadership in Afghanistan: Identifying and assessing determining factors* (Order No. 10587685). ProQuest Dissertations & Theses Global. (1885103267).

Redfield, R., Linton, R., & Hersokivitz, M. (1936). Memorandum for the study of acculturation. *American Anthropologist, 38*(1), 149-152.

Rickert, J. (2012). Patient-centered care: What it means and how to get there. *Health Affairs*. https://www.healthaffairs.org/do/10.1377/hblog20120124.016506/full/

Rigoloski, E. (2013). *Management and leadership in nursing and health care: An experiential approach.* New York: Springer Publishing Co.

Rogers, D. M. (2017). *Emergence of informal clinical leadership among bedside nurses in the acute care clinical setting: A mixed methods study* (Order No. 10638387). ProQuest Dissertations & Theses Global.

Ross, C. (2014). The benefits of informal leadership. *Nurse Leader, 12*(5), 68-70.

Rudman, L. A., & Glick, P. (2010). *The social psychology of gender: How power and intimacy shape gender relations.* New York, NY: The Guilford press.

Sadat, M. H. (2008). Hyphenating Afghaniyat (Afghan-ness) in the Afghan diaspora. *Journal of Muslim Minority Affairs, 28*(3), 329-342. doi:10.1080/13602000802547898

Schermerhorn, J. R., Hunt, J. G., & Osborn, R. (2008). *Organizational behavior* (10th ed.). Hoboken: John Wiley & Sons, Inc.

Schmitt, D., Long, A., McPhearson, A., O'Brien, K., Remmert, B., and Shah, S. (2017). Personality and gender differences in global perspective. *International Journal of Psychology*, *52*(S1), 45-56.

Scully, J. N. (2015). Leadership in nursing: The importance of recognizing inherent values and attributes to secure a positive future for the profession. *Collegian*, *22*(4), 439-444.

Sfantou, D. F., Laliotis, A., Patelarou, A. E., Sifaki- Pistolla, D., Matalliotakis, M., Patelarou, E. (2017). Importance of leadership style towards quality of care measures in healthcare Settings: A systematic review. *Healthcare, 5*(73) 1-17.

Shi, L., Lee, D., Chung, M., Liang, H., Lock, D., & Sripopatana, A. (2018). Patient-centered medical home recognition and clinical performance in U.S. community health centers. *Health Services Research*, *52*(3), 984-1004.

Sherwood, A., & DePaolo, C. (2005). Task and relationship-oriented trust in leaders. *Journal of Leadership and Organization Studies*, *12*(2), 65-81.

Smith, K. B., Profetto-McGrath, J., & Cummings, G. G. (2009). Emotional intelligence and nursing: An integrative literature review. *International Journal of Nursing*, *46*(12), 1624-1636.

Snaebjornsson, I. M., Edvardsson, I. R., Zydziunaite, V., & Vaiman, V. (2015). *SAGE open: Cross-cultural leadership.* Sage Publications. oi:10.1177/2158244015579727

Sonnino R. E. (2016). Health care leadership development and training: Progress and pitfalls. *Journal of Healthcare Leadership*, *8*, 19–29.

Stefl, M. E. (2008). Common competencies for all healthcare managers: The healthcare leadership alliance model. *Journal of Healthcare Management*, *53*(6), 360-374.

Steenkamp, J. E. M., (2001). The role of national culture in international marketing research, *International Marketing Review*, *18*(1), 30-44.

Stempel, C., Sami, N., Koga, P. M., Alemi, Q., Smith, V., & Shirazi, A. (2016). Gendered sources of distress and resilience among Afghan refugees in Northern California: A cross-sectional Study. *International Journal of Environmental Research and Public Health, 14*(1), 1-22.

Tabachnick, B. G., & Fidell, L. S. (2019). *Using multivariate statistics* (7th ed.). Boston, MA: Pearson.

Tajaddini, R. & Mujtaba, B. G. (2010). Stress and leadership tendencies of respondents from Iran: Exploring similarities and differences based on age and gender. *Public Organization Review, 11*, 219-236.

Talwar, G. (2012). *The experiences of male Afghan refugees in the United States, seen through the lens of Sarbin's social role theory* (Order No. 10289893). ProQuest Dissertations & Theses Global. (1862554861).

Talwar, G. (2014). *Acculturation, construction of gender and social identity in a sample of Afghan immigrants in the U.S* (Order No. 3668754). ProQuest Dissertations & Theses Global. (1648398567).

Tang, M. (2019). *Career development and counseling: Theory and practice in a multicultural world*. Thousand Oaks, CA: SAGE Publications, Inc.

Tannenbaum, C., Greaves, L., & Graham, I. (2016). Why sex and gender matter in implementation research. *BMC Medical Research Methodology, 16*(145), 1-9.

Tesluk, P. E., & Jacobs, R. R. (1998). Toward an integrated model of work experience. *Personnel Psychology, 51*, 321–355.

Tjosvold, D., & Leung, K. (2016). *Cross-cultural management: Foundations and future*. London: Routledge.

TradeArabia. (2018). Arabian healthcare teams up with US group. *Trade Arabia*. http://tradearabia.com/news/HEAL_337693.html

Trevino, D. (2010). *Acculturation and leadership styles of elected Latino leaders* (Order No. 3411402). ProQuest Dissertations & Theses Global. (527854489).

Triandis, H. C. (1988). *Collectivism vs. individualism: A reconceptualization of a basic concept in cross-cultural social psychology*, in Verma, G. K. and Bagley, C., (Eds.), Cross-Cultural Studies of Personality, Attitudes and Cognition. Macmillan, London, 60-95.

Vandayani, P., Kartini, D., Hilmiana, H., & Azis, Y. (2015). The impact of national culture on effectiveness of situational leadership Hersey–Blanchard. *International Journal of Scientific & Technology Research*, *4*(7), 78–82.

Vertovec, S. (1999). Conceiving and researching transnationalism. *Ethnic and Racial Studies*, *22*, 447–462.

Weatherby, J. N., Arceneaux, C., Evans, E. B., Long, D., Reed, I., & Novika-Carter, O. D. (2009). *The other world: Issues and politics of the developing world* (8th ed.). New York, NY: Pearson.

West, M., Smithgall, L., Rosler, G., & Winn, E. (2016). Evaluation of a nurse leadership development program. *Nursing Management, 22*(10), 26-28.

Wheatley, B. (2010). *Leadership styles of healthcare executives: Comparisons of transformational, transactional, and passive-avoidant styles*. ProQuest Dissertations and Theses database.

White, P. (2009). *Developing research questions: A guide for social scientists*. New York: Palgrave.

Wise, S. (2019). Has the search for better leadership come at the expense of management? *International Journal of Nursing Studies*, *97*, A1–A2.

Wren, J. T. (1995). *The leader's companion: Insights on leadership through the ages*. New York, NY: The Free Press.

Wright, J. (2013). How foreign-born graduates impact the STEM workforce shortage debate. *Forbes*. https://www.forbes.com/sites/emsi/2013/05/28/how-foreign-born-graduates-impact-the-stem-worker-shortage-debate/#41ddf4c91b96

Wyatt, J. (2015). Healthcare management and leadership. *Perspectives in Public Health, 135*(5), 222.

Xu, L., Chi, I., & Wu, S. (2018). Grandparent–grandchild relationships in Chinese immigrant families in Los Angeles: Roles of acculturation and the middle generation. *Gerontology and Geriatric Medicine, 4*, 1-8.

Zong, J., Batalova, J., and Hallock, J. (2018). Frequently requested statistics on immigrants and immigration in the United States. *Migration Policy.* https://www.migrationpolicy.org/article/frequently-requested-statistics-immigrants-and-immigration-united-states

Zoppi, I. M. (2004). *The relationship of self-perceived leadership style and acculturation of Latinas in the United States Army* (Order No. 3152509). ProQuest Dissertations & Theses Global. (305176366).

APPENDICES

Appendix A: IRB Explanation

Review of Graduate Student Research by the Institutional Review Board (IRB)

What is the IRB?

The IRB is a committee of scientists, non-scientists and community members. At many universities, the IRB reviews research proposals to protect the rights and welfare of human research subjects who participate in research activities conducted under the auspices of the University.

When is IRB review required?

If the proposed study meets the federal definition of research…

"A systematic investigation, including research development, testing and evaluation, designed to develop or contribute to generalizable knowledge and if the proposed study involves "human subjects," defined as "a living individual about whom an investigator (whether professional or student) conducting research obtains: 1) data through intervention or interaction with the individual; or 2) identifiable private information."

Why is IRB review necessary?

IRB reviews help ensure the safety and protection of research subjects, as well as the ethical conduct of research that involves human subjects.

The IRB review must determine that all of the following requirements are satisfied.

- Risks to subjects are minimized.
- Risks to subjects are reasonable in relation to anticipated benefits.
- Selection of subjects is equitable.
- Informed consent will be sought from each prospective subject or the subject's legally authorized representative.
- Informed consent will be appropriately documented, in accordance with, and to the extent required by HSS regulation 46.117.
- The research plan makes adequate provision for the monitoring of data collected to ensure the safety of subjects.
- There are adequate provisions to protect the privacy of subjects and to maintain the confidentiality of data. When some or all of the subjects are likely to be vulnerable to coercion or undue influence, such as children, prisoners, pregnant women, mentally disabled persons or economically disadvantaged persons, additional safeguards have been included in the study to protect the rights and welfare of these subjects.

125

Appendix B: Invitation to Participate—Leader Orientation Study

Dear Participant:

Please consider this invitation to participate in a research study. The intent of this study is to examine the approach to leadership among Afghan descent who work in the US healthcare system as registered nurses. You do not have to hold a leadership position to participate. All you need to quality is to be of Afghan decent over 18 years of age who is a Nurse in the US healthcare system.

Your participation in this study will provide healthcare leaders and scholars with greater understanding of the influence of acculturation on leadership. The results from this survey may be used to develop leadership strategies designed to tailor opportunities for people of Afghan descent to climb the corporate ladder.

Please feel free to send this Invitation to your colleagues who meet the requirements of this study and who may want to participate in this study.

To participate, please click the link to the survey below. Participation takes about 5-15 minutes. Your participation is completely confidential. Your information will be protected from disclosure and contact information will not be retained.

Your complete and honest participation is very important to the success of this research and I appreciate your help. If you have any questions, please contact me at: belalkaifi@_____.

Sincerely,

Belal Kaifi

Appendix C: Nurse Acculturation and Leadership Survey

1. Are you at least 18 years old? ☐ Yes   ☐ No [If no, does not continue with survey]

2. Were one or both of your parents originally from Afghanistan? ☐ Yes ☐ No
   [If no, does not continue with survey]

3. Are you a registered nurse currently practicing in the US Health System? ☐ Yes ☐ No
   [If no, does not continue with survey]

4. What year were you born? _____

5. Where were you born? ☐ US ☐ Afghanistan ☐ Other (please report the country of

   birth_____

6. How many years have you worked as a nurse in healthcare? _____

7. What is your job title? Please choose one of the following

   ☐ – Registered Nurse
   ☐ – Certified Registered Nurse Anesthetist
   ☐ - Nurse Practitioner
   ☐ - Other Nurse (Please Specify) _____
8. What is your sex? ☐ Male   ☐ Female

9. What is your highest educational level completed?

   ☐ 2-Yr College Degree (Associate of Science in Nursing)

   ☐ 4-Yr College Degree (Bachelor of Science in Nursing)

   ☐ Graduate School Degree (Master of Science in Nursing)

   ☐ Other Education (Please Specify) _____

For survey items 10-29, please choose one number between 1 and 5 indicate how often you engage in the stated behavior.
1 = never, 2 = occasionally, 3 = sometimes, 4 = frequently, 5 = always

10. Tells group members what they are supposed to do.

11. Sets standards of performance for group members.

12. Makes suggestions about how to solve problems.

13. Makes his or her perspective clear to others.

14. Develops a plan of action for the group.

15. Defines role responsibilities for each group member.

16. Clarifies his or her own role within the group.

17. Provides a plan for how the work is to be done.

18. Provides criteria for what is expected of the group.

19. Encourages group members to do high-quality work.

20. Acts friendly with members of the group.

21. Helps others feel comfortable in the group.

22. Responds favorably to suggestions made by others.

23. Treats others fairly.

24. Behaves in a predictable manner toward group members.

25. Communicates actively with group members.

26. Shows concern for the well-being of others.

27. Shows flexibility in making decisions.

28. Discloses thoughts and feelings to group members.

29. Helps group members get along.

For survey items 30-53, please choose one number between 1 and 5 that indicates how often you engage in the stated behavior:

(1 = not at all, 2 = very little or not very often, 3 = moderately, 4 = more or very often, 5 = extremely often or almost always).

30. I speak English.

31. My thinking is done in the English language.

32. I enjoy reading in English (e.g. books).

33. I write in English.

34. I enjoy English language movies.

35. I associate with White Americans.

36. I enjoy listening to English language music.

37. My friends now are of White (specific) origin.

38. I enjoy English language TV.

39. My friends while I was growing up were of White origin.

40. I like to identify myself as an American.

41. My contact with the USA has been (not at all < -- > almost always).

42. I associate with Afghans and/or Afghan Americans.

43. I enjoy listening to Afghan language music.

44. I enjoy Dari/Pashto language TV and movies.

45. My friends now are of Afghan origin.

46. My family cooks Afghan food.

47. I write/read in Dari/Pashto (e.g. letters and books).

48. I speak Dari/Pashto.

49. My thinking is done in the Dari/Pashto language.

50. My contact with Afghanistan has been (not at all < -- > almost always).

51. My friends while I was growing up were of Afghan origin.

52. I enjoy speaking Dari/Pashto.

53. I like to identify myself as an Afghan.

Appendix D: Afghanistan Government Research Support Letter

Letter of support for this research study from Deputy Minister Rohullah Niazi of the Independent Directorate of Local Governance, Government of Islamic Republic of Afghanistan.

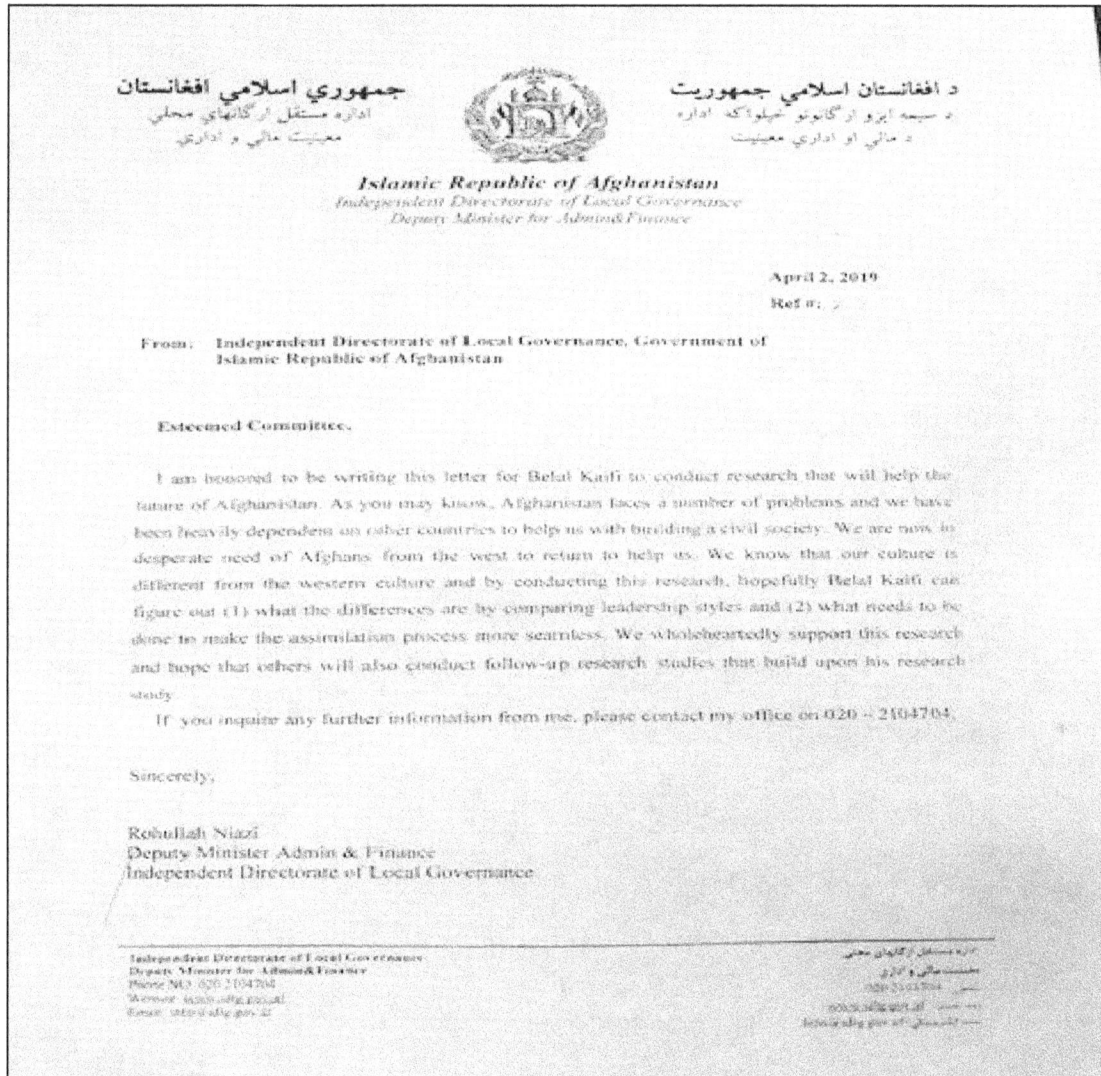

جمهوري اسلامي افغانستان
اداره مستقل ارگانهاي محلي
معینیت مالي و اداري

د افغانستان اسلامي جمهوريت
د سيمه ايزو ارگانونو خپلواکه اداره
د مالي او اداري معینیت

Islamic Republic of Afghanistan
Independent Directorate of Local Governance
Deputy Minister for Admin & Finance

April 2, 2019
Ref #:

From: Independent Directorate of Local Governance, Government of
         Islamic Republic of Afghanistan

Esteemed Committee,

I am honored to be writing this letter for Belal Kaifi to conduct research that will help the future of Afghanistan. As you may know, Afghanistan faces a number of problems and we have been heavily dependent on other countries to help us with building a civil society. We are now in desperate need of Afghans from the west to return to help us. We know that our culture is different from the western culture and by conducting this research, hopefully Belal Kaifi can figure out (1) what the differences are by comparing leadership styles and (2) what needs to be done to make the assimilation process more seamless. We wholeheartedly support this research and hope that others will also conduct follow-up research studies that build upon his research study.

If you inquire any further information from me, please contact my office on 020 – 2104704.

Sincerely,

Rohullah Niazi
Deputy Minister Admin & Finance
Independent Directorate of Local Governance

Independent Directorate of Local Governance
Deputy Minister for Admin&Finance
Phone NO: 020 2104704
Website: idlg.idlg.gov.af
Email: info@idlg.gov.af

Appendix E: Leadership Style Questionnaire (LSQ) Author Research Support Message

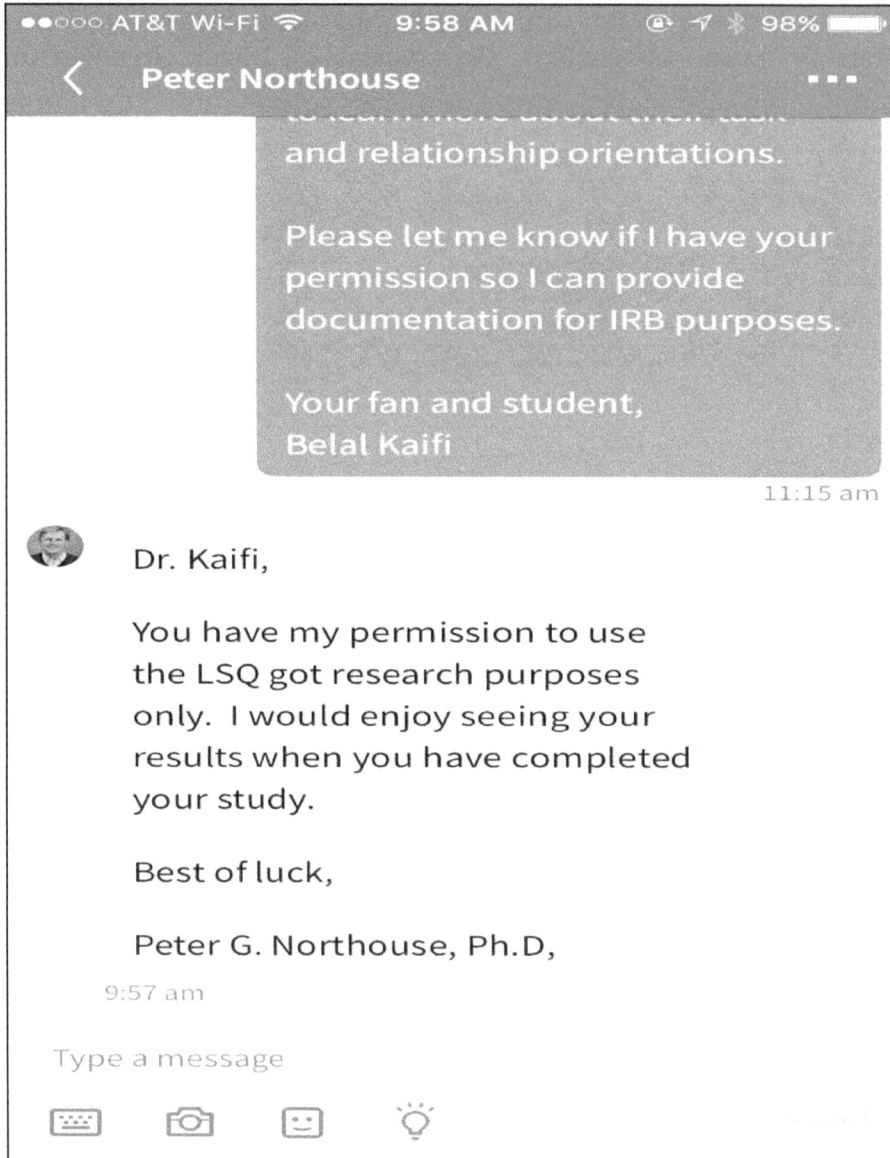

and relationship orientations.

Please let me know if I have your permission so I can provide documentation for IRB purposes.

Your fan and student,
Belal Kaifi

11:15 am

Dr. Kaifi,

You have my permission to use the LSQ got research purposes only. I would enjoy seeing your results when you have completed your study.

Best of luck,

Peter G. Northouse, Ph.D,

9:57 am

Type a message

Appendix F: Leadership Style Questionnaire (LSQ) Use Permission

RE: Permission to use Leadership Style Questionnaire (LSQ)

Dear Belal Kaifi,

Thank you for your request. I am pleased to report we can grant your request without a fee as part of your thesis or dissertation.

Please accept this email as permission for your request as you've detailed below. Permission is granted for the life of the edition on a non-exclusive basis, in the English language, throughout the world in all formats provided full citation is made to the original SAGE publication. Permission does not include any third-party material found within the work. Please contact us for any further usage of the material.

If you have any questions, or if we may be of further assistance, please let us know.

Kind Regards,
Mary

Rights Coordinator

SAGE Publishing

Appendix G: ARSMA-II Use Permission

RE: Requesting Copyright Permission for Cuellar's ARSMA-II

To: Belal Kaifi

Dear Belal,

Thank you for the information. I am pleased to report we can grant your request without a fee as part of your thesis or dissertation.

Please accept this email as permission for your request as you've detailed below. Permission is granted for the life of the edition on a non-exclusive basis, in the English language, throughout the world in all formats provided full citation is made to the original SAGE publication (Cuéllar, I., Arnold, B., & Maldonado, R. (1995). Permission does not include any third-party material found within the work.

Any other type of reproduction or distribution of the questionnaire content is not authorized without additional written permission from SAGE.

 Best Regards,

 Mary

Rights Coordinator

SAGE Publishing

Appendix H: Informed Consent

You are cordially invited to take part in a study that examines the dominant leadership orientation of people of Afghan descent working in healthcare. To qualify, you must be an Afghan American registered nurse over 18 years old (you do not have to hold a leadership position). This form provides informed consent information that allows you to understand this study before deciding whether to take part in it.

This study is being conducted by researcher Belal Kaifi.

PURPOSE OF THE STUDY: To determine the dominant leadership orientation of people of Afghan descent working in healthcare and assess if it relates to exposure to different cultures.

PROCEDURES: If you agree to participate in this study, you will be asked to complete a short survey of 61 questions, which takes an estimated 5-15 minutes to complete.

POTENTIAL RISKS: Your participation does not pose risks to your safety or wellbeing.

POTENTIAL BENEFITS: The benefits of your participation include the chance to reflect on your personal style of leadership within your current organization. As a participant, you are also contributing to the body of knowledge regarding workplace leadership and cross-cultural training. Your information may help develop organizational initiatives to improve leadership trainings that provide more opportunities for Afghan descendants and eventually for individuals from different cultures to ascend the corporate ladder.

PAYMENT FOR PARTICIPATION: There is no monetary incentive for participating in this study.

CONFIDENTIALITY: All your information will be kept confidential and only used for this study. The survey responses will be stored electronically on the researcher's password-protected computer for a period of 5 years, as required by the Internal Review Board. You understand that the results of this research study may be presented at scientific or professional meetings or published in scientific journals.

PARTICIPATION AND WITHDRAWAL: Your participation is voluntary. You have the right to withdraw consent or discontinue participation at any time without penalty or loss of benefits to which you are otherwise entitled.

To withdraw from this study, simply do not complete the survey. Partially completed questionnaires will automatically be eliminated from this study so there is no link to personal identifying information.

CONTACTS AND QUESTIONS: You may ask any questions you have now. Or if you have questions later, you may contact:

135

Belal A. Kaifi
belalkaifi@_____ .

If you have questions regarding your rights as a research subject, contact the Institutional Review Board for the Protection of Human Subjects.

STATEMENT OF CONSENT I have read and understand the above information above and (choose one):

[ ] I agree to participate

[ ] I do not agree to participate

About the Author

Dr. Belal A. Kaifi completed a post-doctoral program in Business Administration with an emphasis in Management and Marketing at the University of Florida (Hough Graduate School of Business - AACSB accredited). He is academically qualified to teach in the departments of Health Care Administration, Business Administration, Public Administration, and Education. Dr. Kaifi completed his first doctoral degree in Organization and Leadership at the University of San Francisco and his second doctoral degree in Health Care Administration and Policy at American InterContinental University. He earned a master's degree in Public Administration with an emphasis in Human Resource Management and a second master's degree in Business Administration. Dr. Kaifi earned a Career and Technical Education (CTE) teaching credential in Business and Finance. His undergraduate degree is in Business Administration with an emphasis in Management.

Dr. Kaifi worked for Kaiser Permanente (one of America's leading health care providers and nonprofit health plans) for five years and also worked as a Director and Interim Dean at a vocational allied health college for five years. He has been teaching undergraduate and graduate students for 15 years. Dr. Kaifi has published over 50 peer-reviewed articles since 2008. This is Dr. Kaifi's fifth book, having previously published the following books:

- *Human Resource Management: An Applied Approach (2014)*
- *Organizational Behavior: Managing and Leading Organizations (2013)*
- *Managing Your Future: An Educational Guide (2010)*
- *The Impact of 9/11 on Afghan American Leaders (2009)*

Dr. Kaifi was a Fulbright Scholar Specialist (sponsored by the United States Department of State's Bureau of Educational and Cultural Affairs) and has extensive experience with cross-cultural management, budget planning and administration, training and succession planning, curriculum design and development, accreditation planning, management development, performance evaluations, leadership training and development, online education, faculty recruitment, program review, student learning outcome (SLO) assessment, and AACSB assurance of learning (AOL) standards. Furthermore, Dr. Kaifi has sat on numerous educational advisory committees, dissertation committees, and faculty councils as well as offered his expertise as a mentor to many younger, less experienced professors over the years.

In his spare time, Dr. Kaifi enjoys traveling and learning about different cultures. Thus far, he has traveled to: Afghanistan, Sweden, Germany, Mexico, France, Saudi Arabia, Canada, and Dubai. He considers himself a global citizen.

www.ingramcontent.com/pod-product-compliance
Lightning Source LLC
Chambersburg PA
CBHW080756300326
41914CB00055B/908